Words can create or destroy relationships. Words can make life brighter or darker. They spread a pall of misery or forge a chain of grief. Words can create an atmosphere of good or evil.

But words are not the only way we communicate. We show love by the way we react to a problem situation, by the way we respond to the felt or expressed needs of others, and by the nuances of our behavior. Love is a language everybody understands, a language that is unfailing. "Love never faileth"
(1 Cor. 13:8).

Quick to Listen,

Slow to Speak

ROBERT E. FISHER

Living Books®
Tyndale House Publishers, Inc.
Wheaton, Illinois

This book was previously published as *The Language of Love: Scriptural Guidelines for Communication* by Robert Fisher.

Unless otherwise indicated, all Scripture quotations are from the *Holy Bible,* New International Version, copyright © 1973, 1978, 1984 by International Bible Society. Used by permission of Zondervan Bible Publishers. Scripture quotations marked TLB are from *The Living Bible,* copyright © 1971 held by assignment by KNT Charitable Trust. All rights reserved. Scripture quotations marked AMP are from *The Amplified Bible.* Old Testament copyright © 1965, 1987 by the Zondervan Corporation. New Testament copyright © 1958, 1987 by the Lockman Foundation. Used by permission. Scripture quotations marked NASB are from the *New American Standard Bible,* copyright © 1960, 1962, 1963, 1968, 1971, 1972, 1973, 1975, 1977 by The Lockman Foundation. Used by permission.

Living Books is a registered trademark of Tyndale House Publishers, Inc.

To my father

H . H A R O L D   F I S H E R

who in his nearly ninety years
of living has exemplified the language of love
as well as anyone I have ever known

CONTENTS

Foreword

Nothing has more power to enrich life or to make life miserable than do relationships. Most Christians struggle with the challenge of building healthier relationships. We all want to know how to structure our words and actions to assure others that we are truly interested in them.

Language can create or destroy relationships. Words can make life brighter or darker. Words can spread a pall of misery or forge a chain of grief. Words can create an atmosphere of good or evil.

But words are not the only way we communicate. We communicate by the way we react to a problem situation, by the way we respond to the felt or expressed needs of others, and by the nuances of our behavior. Communication is a multifaceted challenge.

Love is a language everybody understands. In

fact, it is a language that is unfailing in all ways. "Love never faileth" (1 Cor. 13:8). All Christian communication must be guided by love.

In this exciting book, Dr. Robert E. Fisher deals with the intricacies and challenges of building right relationships. He asserts, without apology, that relationships do matter to our spiritual well-being, that intimacy is necessary to the Christian life, and that a caring life is essential to one's physical, psychological, and spiritual well-being.

Dr. Fisher is uniquely qualified, both academically and spiritually, to deal with this important subject. His academic training with a doctorate in counseling psychology and his God-given insight into the scriptural principles for effective communication contribute to make this book extremely readable and practical in the everydayness of life — in cultivating, sustaining, and healing relationships.

Robert Fisher has demonstrated in real life that he knows about that which he writes. He has made a habit of practicing the scriptural guidelines which are featured in this book. We know that firsthand as friends and colleagues in ministry.

Carl Richardson
Lamar Vest

Preface

From earliest childhood I can remember sensing the effect of communication—verbal and nonverbal—upon the character of relationships.

I recall in my preschool years the warmth of a loving relationship with my mother that was nurtured through a nightly ritual of my snuggling in her lap while she hugged me, told me she loved me, rocked me, and sang me to sleep. Even today when I sing some words like, "There's a long, long trail a-winding into the land of my dreams," I feel again the satisfying security of a mother-son relationship that taught me early the true meaning of love.

In later years, being the youngest of four brothers, I often ended up being the observer of family interaction rather than a primary participator. This position allowed me to witness firsthand the powerful impact of the various levels of communication as I saw them demonstrated in my own family. When I think about it, I can sense again the stab of pain I felt when angry, critical words were exchanged between people I loved. And I can remember well the rush of joy I experienced when there was a laughing togetherness or a tearful reconciliation.

My personal encounter with Christ and subsequent call to the ministry caused me to become even more aware of the importance of communication to the development of relationships. After attending Bible college and later taking a bachelor's degree in English, the opportunity arose to do graduate work in psychology. The study of human behavior at this level confirmed what I had learned from my early relationships and what the Lord had been showing me after I became a Christian. My doctoral studies gave me the privilege of looking closely at the implications of Jesus' command to "love your neighbor as yourself."

In recent years God used these studies, along with a rewarding involvement in the pastoral and counseling ministries, to impress upon me the primary importance of right relationships—with God and with man. I also came to realize that in building right relationships we have no more useful tool than proper communication.

For the past several years, I have been developing the scriptural guidelines for effective communication that are the basis for this book. As I have continued through this study, I have been constantly amazed to see how perfectly and practically God's

Word speaks to the problems of interpersonal communication. Nowhere is the description of the Word as "quick [alive] and powerful" more apt than in this area of human behavior.

Every time I have preached or taught on this subject, I have seen the truth of God set captives free. Following a recent seminar session, a successful businessman who had experienced some traumatic family problems spoke to me with tears flowing down his cheeks. "I didn't realize until today," he said, "how flagrantly I have been disobeying the Word of God in my family relationships. I see now that most of the problems in my family have been a result of my disobedience. With God's help that is going to change!"

The idea for a book on this subject grew out of the many requests for a more detailed presentation. With strong encouragement from family and friends the project was undertaken.

The title of the series, *The Language of Love,* emerged from a twofold conviction: (1) Communication is composed of many elements, both verbal and nonverbal, which are embodied in a total interpersonal language; and (2) the most effective vehicle to convey that language is love.

In an undertaking like this there are always many persons to whom thanks is due. The first that comes to mind is my wife, Mary, who helps me understand and practice (though still imperfectly) these principles through her loving care and confidence. Also, to my three children, Bob, Cameron, and Lorri, for their willingness to put up with a father who is still struggling to speak more consistently the language of love. Special notes of appreciation go to Floyd Carey for his prodding, positive encouragement; to Carl Richardson and Lamar Vest for their strengthening friendship; and to Karen Hutchinson, my personal secretary, for her many hours of faithful work in typing the manuscript.

May this feeble attempt to articulate and apply the powerful truths of Scripture give some added insight and strength to all who have a desire to speak more perfectly the language of love.

A Note from the Editor

SOME PRACTICAL WAYS TO USE THIS BOOK

Individual Study. At the beginning of each chapter you will find a guideline with several Scripture verses to help you reinforce the message of that chapter. After you have read the book in its entirety, return to the beginning and, taking one chapter a week, memorize the Scripture verses given in the guideline for that week.

Family Study. For the next ten weeks, consider using the book as part of your family devotions, reading a short section from the chapter each day. Notice that the guidelines at the beginning of each chapter are marked with dotted lines to enable you to cut out the page for other uses. If you are studying one chapter per week, consider taping the guideline in a prominent place, perhaps on the refrigerator door, so everyone in the family can see it.

Creative Family Exercise. Try to think of some creative ways that you and your family can, using the guideline for the week, reinforce the message of each chapter. For instance, post a chart listing all the family members. During the week, anyone in the family who recognizes another family member putting into practice the guideline for the week gets a star for himself and a star for the person who demonstrated the "language of love." Recognizing good traits in others affirms them and also encourages positive behavior in those around them.

Love

Stop Talking and Start Listening

My dear brothers, take note of this: Everyone should be quick to listen, slow to speak and slow to become angry.

James 1:19

He who answers before listening—that is his folly and his shame.

Proverbs 18:13

O N E
Stop Talking and Start Listening

When I was first called to the ministry, I wondered if God had made a mistake. Not only could I not preach, I had great difficulty even in carrying on a decent conversation. When I was with a group of friends or, worse yet, on a date with a girl I was trying to impress, I struggled to think of something brilliant or humorous to say. Usually the thought never came. My idea of a good conversation was one in which I talked with ease while everyone else listened with admiration.

Right after I went away to college to study for the ministry, someone gave me a book by Dale Carnegie, *How to Win Friends and Influence People.* It turned out to be a very popular book—reportedly selling more copies in the English language than any other book but the Bible. The chapter that interested me most was entitled, "An Easy Way to Become a

Good Conversationalist." To my surprise, Carnegie gave a rule that was just the opposite of what I supposed to be true. To become a good conversationalist, he said, one must first become a good listener. Others are not nearly as interested in what we have to say as they are in what they want to say to us.

What a paradoxical idea! According to Carnegie, good conversation is determined more by how well we listen than how well we speak.

The school I was attending at that time was about 250 miles from where my girlfriend lived. Since I had to sell my car to pay my college tuition, the only way I could see Mary every few weeks was to hitchhike my way down Highway 99 from Fresno to Corona, California. After reading Carnegie's book, I decided that on my next trip to southern California I would put into practice his rule for good conversation with every person who picked me up.

Early the next Saturday morning, I was out on the highway. A car finally pulled over. The driver said he could take me as far as Bakersfield — about a hundred miles down the road. As we began the journey together, he started talking and I started listening. To my surprise, as I paid close attention to what he was saying, I found myself genuinely interested and involved in the conversation. Occasionally I would make a comment or ask a pertinent question, but I was never asked and never gave any information about myself.

The time passed quickly, and soon we were in Bakersfield. We came to the crossroads where my friend was to turn off. Instead, he decided to take me to another main intersection ten miles or so farther, to where he thought my chances for getting a ride would be better. As we traveled on, he kept talking and I kept listening. When we arrived at our new destination, he remarked that he had never seen so few cars on the road. I might have a difficult time getting picked up there, he said, so he would take me to the base of the Ridge Route, where the mountain range separated the central and southern part of the state. That was another fifteen miles. He kept talking; I kept listening.

As we came to the Ridge Route he had to make a decision. Was he going to take me over the mountain into southern California (about seventy-five miles) or was he going to let me out, turn around, and go back home?

"I can't believe this traffic," he said. "You know, I don't have anything important to do today. I'm going to take you on over the mountain." He couldn't believe the traffic; I couldn't believe what this man was doing for me. An hour or so later we arrived in the San Fernando Valley.

"Tell me, where is this town your girlfriend lives in?" he asked. I told him it was another sixty miles or so off the main highway.

"What's the difference," he said. "I've come this far; I might as well take you all the way."

During all our time together, he had never asked me anything about myself—not even my name. He had told me about his family, his business, his dreams and ambitions. I forgot about trying to impress him by telling him about myself. I found it interesting and stimulating to learn so much about another person. I thoroughly enjoyed the conversation.

He took me right to Mary's front door. Unbelievable! I thanked him profusely for his kindness and generosity. As I got out and was about to close the car door, he stopped me.

"Just a minute, young man. Before you go I want to tell you something. I make a habit of picking up hitchhikers. I like to learn about other people. I enjoy a good conversation." He paused and became more serious. "I know you're young," he said, "but I want you to know you are absolutely one of the finest conversationalists I have ever met."

I learned a lesson of life that day I will never forget. I learned the joy of listening, but perhaps more importantly, I learned the value of controlling my own tongue for a positive purpose.

THE DANGER OF TALKING

Most of us talk too much. If God were to speak to us in plain terms about our communication with others, he probably would say, "Learn to keep your mouth closed!" The more we talk, the greater the possibility of our sinning (Prov. 10:19). The simple truth is that when we are talking, we cannot be listening. Someone has observed that God created us with *two* ears and *one* mouth, perhaps a clue that we should listen twice as much as we speak.

Shakespeare wrote, "Give every man thine ear, but few thy voice."

The Bible admonishes, "Be quick to listen [and] slow to speak" (James 1:19). Usually in our communication with others, we reverse that order. We are quick to speak and slow to listen. We want to say what we want to say and are impatient when others wish to express their point of view. No behavior on our part is more self-centered than the demand to speak and the refusal to listen. Such behavior is a root cause of most interpersonal conflict.

In counseling sessions with couples experiencing marital difficulties, I usually set an important guideline at the outset of the discussion. I suggest that the wife first say what she wants to say without interruption from her husband. When she finishes, the husband is to express his perspective of the problem while his wife listens. The result of this arrangement can be quite revealing.

Often the wife, after beginning to tell her side of the story, will become too emotional to continue. She will say something like this: "Do you know, this is the first time since our marriage got into trouble that my husband has heard what I have to say. He always avoids the issue; he never listens to me."

The reaction from the husband is similar: "I've tried to talk to her about these things, but she always gets upset. She never lets me explain."

The infamous "generation gap" is caused primarily by a failure of parent and child to listen to one another.

When we listen, we learn. How often have I heard one mate say to another after one of those periods of "forced" listening, "I never knew you felt that way," to which the usual response is, "I've been trying to tell you for years."

The fact is when we are talking, we are learning nothing about one another. It is paradoxical that we think we know each other so well, especially those in our own family. "I know her like a book," the husband says of his wife. The only problem is he has never taken the time to read the book.

In her novel, *Corinne*, written in 1807, the famous Franco-Swiss woman of letters Madame de Stael penned a line that has been variously translated and often quoted: "To know all is to forgive all." Studies of the dynamics of human relationships have shown that generally the better we know each other, the better we get along. Conflict (as well as prejudice and bigotry) is a by-product of a lack of knowledge of others. On the other hand, the more we perceive the other person as he perceives himself, the more likely we are to have a positive relationship with him. The best way for us to understand how another person feels or thinks or how he perceives himself is to let him tell us. That is not possible when we are doing most of the talking. Nixon Waterman expressed this idea in his poem, "To Know All Is to Forgive All."

If I knew you and you knew me —
If both of us could clearly see,
And with an inner sight divine

The meaning of your heart and mine —
I'm sure that we would differ less
And clasp our hands in friendliness;
Our thoughts would pleasantly agree
If I knew you, and you knew me.

If I knew you and you knew me,
As each one knows his own self, we
Could look each other in the face
And see therein a truer grace.
Life has so many hidden woes,
So many thorns for every rose;
The "why" of things our hearts would see,
If I knew you and you knew me.

Most of us must force ourselves to become better listeners. The first step, of course, is to limit our talking. However, less talking must always be coupled with more and better listening. To limit talking without increasing listening is to exacerbate the problem. That is why the Bible gives the simple formula: "Be quick to listen [and] slow to speak."

When we listen, we love. One of the most comforting thoughts about God is his willingness to listen. His ear is not so heavy that he cannot hear (Isa. 59:1). His ear is open to the cries of his people (Ps. 34:15). We say we know God loves us because he pays attention to us. He not only allows us to talk with him, he urges us to do so. And we have the assurance that when we speak to him, he hears us and he understands. There is great satisfaction in being able to tell God how we feel.

If this characteristic of God is so important to our relationship with him, why is it we have such a difficult time applying that same principle to our relationships with others? Too often we operate on the notion that verbalizing our love is all we need to do to maintain a relationship.

In these days, particularly in Christian circles, we find it very easy to say, "I love you." It is a basic scriptural truth that love is *not* something you say, but something you do. First Corinthians 13 is a litany of the "acts" of love. There is no more powerful way to demonstrate our love one for another than by being quick to listen and slow to speak.

In a practical sense, a husband must consciously take time to listen to his wife. He must do so (at least initially) without a defense of his own position or an explanation of his perspective. A wife must give her husband the chance to express his point of view without her becoming accusatory or emotionally upset. A child deserves the right to be heard patiently and intently by his parents without belittlement or condemnation. As God's ear is open to us, our ear must be open to others. And an open ear generally presupposes a closed mouth.

I have said that this book is mostly about how to keep your mouth closed. In almost every instance when God talks about our communication with others, he notes the need for restraint and control of our tongue. However, in an effort to strike a scriptural balance, this book is also about how to be a good listener. According to the Scriptures, communication is primarily a matter of listening.

THE ART OF LISTENING

It is not enough just to listen; we must listen in the right way—with the right motivation and attitude. Although the Bible doesn't use the term "listen" frequently, it speaks volumes about "hearing." The message is simple: "He that has ears, let him hear." God commands us to be good listeners.

One of the first things God tells us about listening is that it is done *intentionally.* In chapters 2 and 3 of the book of Revelation, John recorded letters to the seven churches of Asia. At the end of each of those letters, he was instructed to record the admonition: "He who has an ear, let him hear what the Spirit says to the churches." The dictionary defines *listening* as a "conscious effort to hear."

Profitable listening does not happen by accident; it is intentional. It is a planned, conscious act of the will. When we listen to God, it is because we must. We understand that it is something vital to our relationship. The same is true of our relationships with others. If we hear them as we should, it will be because we intended it that way.

Proper communication between husband and wife depends upon specific times of listening to one another. It cannot be stressed too strongly that these must be planned times, arbitrarily fitted into personal schedules. If this is not done, generally one of two things will happen: there will be little or no listening at all, or stress and resentment will build up and force a destructive kind of dialogue.

The husband as the head of the home should take the lead in this intentional listening process. If the husband does not take the initiative, then the wife should approach him. The temptation is always to talk rather than listen. Keep in mind that the idea is to be "quick to *listen*." Leading questions such as "Tell me how you feel about this situation" or "What are your ideas on this matter?" will get the conversation started in the right direction.

Often children feel that parents will not listen to them. On a one-to-one basis, at specifically planned times, every son and daughter should be given the opportunity to express his or her opinions and feelings to an attentive mom and dad. Another good idea, when children get a little older, is to convene family meetings where every family member has a chance to be heard. Children who are listened to by their parents are much more apt to be open to instruction from their parents.

Listening should also be done *attentively.* Another definition of *listening* is to "attend closely." Few things are more disillusioning and disconcerting than to put up with an inattentive listener. Listening time should be quality time. Distractions should be kept to a minimum. Good eye contact should be maintained. Pertinent questions should be asked when appropriate. A well-intentioned time of communication can be ruined if some of these simple rules are not observed.

Attention translates into love. David wondered at the love of God when he mused: "When I consider your heavens, the work of your fingers, the moon and the stars, which you have set in place, what is man that you are mindful of him, the son of man that you care for him? You made him a little lower than the heavenly beings and crowned him with glory and honor" (Ps. 8:3-5). We know God pays attention to us because he loves us. A husband, wife, son, daughter, or friend knows the same thing. We pay attention to those we love. Unfortunately, we don't seem to understand sometimes that the reverse of that is also true—when we fail to pay attention, when we fail to listen, we are perceived as not loving.

Rapt and exclusive attention is one of the greatest gifts we can give another individual. It is the highest form of compliment.

Listening should also be done *understandingly.* We must listen with an open heart. If we are not careful, we will listen *defensively,* mentally making notes of what we can say in return to defend ourselves. When this happens, it is unlikely we will grasp the true meaning of what is being said. The real message will be lost because we are filtering it through our own defense system.

Skillful listening involves a determined effort to perceive the context from which the other person is speaking. In a biblical sense we must practice spiritual discernment (1 Cor. 2:14; 12:10); we must know the other person "after the Spirit." Paul wrote, "So from now on we regard no one from a worldly point of view. Though we once regarded Christ in this way, we do so no longer" (2 Cor. 5:16). Jesus was practicing this principle when, in his last agonizing moments on the cross, he heard the cries and curses of the people, and responded, "Father, forgive them, for they do not know what they are doing" (Luke 23:34).

When emotions are pent up, when the body is tired or afflicted, when the mind is in anguish — these conditions have a direct bearing on how a person expresses himself. An understanding listener will take these facts into consideration.

Finally, listening should be done *actively*. By that I mean what is said should be acted upon and not quickly forgotten. Note is made of important points and there is follow-through where necessary. Again, *listen* is defined as "to give heed or take advice."

The Bible indicates that listening as we should will cause us to act positively. We are told to hear and have mercy (Ps. 30:10), hear and be wise (Prov. 8:33), hear and do (James 1:23). Active listening will not allow what we hear to go in one ear and out the other. As we listen to what the other person is saying, we will be moved to change our behavior toward him or her in a more positive and productive way.

We listen to others so we can learn better how to relate to them. If that goal is to be achieved, listening must be done often and in depth. It must become as natural a response as talking. For most of us, that is a tall order. We have been programmed to believe that the best way to communicate is for us to do the talking. We have a difficult time keeping the bridle on our tongue.

THE FOLLY OF INTERRUPTION

To get our word in, even if it is edgewise, seems to be a major goal of most of us. Some people have a knack for dominating a conversation, either by the level of their volume or the volume of their words—or both. We "ordinary" people have to jump into a conversation where we can. That can adversely affect the way we listen. Often the quality of our listening is poor because we spend most of our time during a conversation thinking about what we are going to say and when we are going to say it.

The low level of listening will eventually cause us to commit some terrible communication blunders. One blunder is to interrupt a person before he is finished speaking. The Bible says, "He who answers before listening—that is his folly and his shame" (Prov. 18:13). Some of us pay the price of folly and shame regularly and don't even realize it.

Interruption creates a number of problems. First, it shows disrespect to the speaker. It indicates disinterest and an unwillingness to listen. All of us have experienced the jarring effect of an interruption while we were speaking. It is tough on our self-esteem. It certainly does nothing to enhance our relationship with the person doing the interrupting.

When such interruptions occur routinely with persons of close association, the result is a combination of anger, frustration, and discouragement. A person who is interrupted often will soon learn it is less painful to avoid conversation with the guilty party whenever possible. In family relationships, a lack of communication because of the problem of interruption can lead to much deeper difficulties.

Answering a matter before it is heard also results in lost information that may be crucial to relationship needs. One of the peculiarities of human nature is that we tend to save the most pertinent information to the last. We sometimes have to work up courage to talk, so it takes time to get to the heart of a matter. It also takes patience on the part of the listener. Many times we have to wait—and wait—for the truth to be revealed. As the farmer waits for the land to yield its valuable crop (James 5:7), so we must be patient listeners if we are to reap the precious fruit of right relationships.

Another problem with interruption is that it draws attention from the speaker and focuses on the interrupter. It is basically a self-serving, egotistical act. It blatantly states, "What I have to say is more important than what you have to say." No wonder God calls it a "folly and shame." Such self-centeredness does nothing to build better relationships. The idea of servanthood and the concept of preferring our brother is never more important than in the area of communication.

God's most basic guideline for communication is: "Stop talking and start listening." If we heed this one simple rule, our associations with other people, especially those closest to us, will be immeasurably more happy and productive. This is the first critical step in speaking the language of love.

LANGUAGE LESSON

For use in individual study or family devotions

1. Try to recall at least two or three recent occasions when you realized *you* were doing more talking than listening in a conversation.

2. Ask yourself, and perhaps share with someone else, why on those occasions you did more talking than listening.

3. Try to think of ways you could have responded to demonstrate the language of love in show during those occasions.

4. Try to imagine how the other person would have responded to you if you had been a better listener.

Love

G U I D E L I N E   2

Think Before You Speak

A *man finds joy in giving an apt reply—and how good is a timely word! . . . The heart of the righteous weighs its answers, but the mouth of the wicked gushes evil.*

Proverbs 15:23, 28

D *o you see a man who speaks in haste? There is more hope for a fool than for him.*

Proverbs 29:20

T W O
Think Before You Speak

Even though the cardinal scriptural rule for communication is to stop talking and start listening, there obviously comes a time when we must speak. This chapter suggests that when we must speak, we should do so only after contemplating the implication of our words; we should think about our answers before we give them. That truth seems so self-evident we may wonder if it is necessary to emphasize it at all. We have only to remember the oft-repeated lament, "I said it before I thought," to understand the strong scriptural indictment of the person who speaks in haste (Prov. 29:20).

When I was a child, sometimes a little friend would offer to share a secret with me. He would say something like this: "If I tell you my secret, will you promise not to tell anybody else in the whole wide world?" Of course, I wanted to hear what he had to say, so I would pluck an imaginary key out of the air, put it to my lips, turn it several times, and then toss it away. That meant my lips were sealed forever. That is, until my next little friend came along.

I don't remember where I learned that gesture, but I have often thought how helpful it would be if I would make a daily practice of locking my mouth and not opening it again until I had something worthwhile to say. David's prayer would be good for us to repeat every morning before we get out of bed: "Set a guard over my mouth, O Lord; keep watch over the door of my lips" (Ps. 141:3). *The Living Bible* puts it in even plainer terms, "Help me, Lord, to keep my mouth shut and my lips sealed." Solomon wrote the same thing a little differently, "Keep your mouth closed and you'll stay out of trouble" (Prov. 21:23, TLB).

THE IMPACT OF WORDS

Words have incredible power. They can hurt or they can heal. They can strike fear or they can bring inexpressible joy. Most of us have a difficult time believing anything we say is powerful, that our words actually impact the lives of others. Yet almost every word we say shapes the thinking of those who hear us. In some way the impact of our words changes their concept of us, of others, of themselves, and ultimately of God. Those who hear us most are the most affected by our words. What an awesome responsibility we have to guard well what comes out of our mouths!

Words can hurt. They are characterized variously as arrows, darts, daggers, and swords. If these powerful instruments are wielded in the wrong way, they can cut, wound, and even kill. They can alienate, isolate, and excoriate. They can divide families and destroy reputations. Yet too often we live under the illusion that others are little affected by our negative verbal behavior.

Words that criticize, judge, or demean are tools of Satan. It is the devil who is called "the accuser of our brothers" (Rev. 12:10). We must be careful we are not guilty of doing his work.

In the family, the significance of relationships makes our use of words even more critical. The words and expressions of a spouse or a parent carry an inestimable weight for good or ill.

During my doctoral training, I worked on the psychiatric ward of a large military hospital. It was there I met Sally, a seventeen-year-old who was under treatment for attempting to kill her father, an army general. One day she was part of a group therapy session that was videotaped. During the session, Sally was very vocal as she described in detail, with apparent glee, her attempt to kill her father with a butcher knife.

Part of the treatment process called for the group to watch the video replay of the therapy session. When the video was shown, Sally sat in the back of the darkened room, behind everyone else. I sat to the side where I could see her reaction to the video tape. At the outset she was laughing and poking fun with the rest of the group as they viewed themselves on the screen.

When the video came to the part where Sally was describing her relationship with her father — how she hated him and wanted him dead — the room became quiet. I watched Sally as her countenance changed and tears began to roll down her cheeks. She saw herself on the screen saying, "If my father were dead, I would dance on his grave." That statement seemed to hit her like a body blow. She doubled over, jumped up, and ran out the door sobbing. I ran after her down the hall and finally caught her where she stopped, facing a wall. I asked her to tell me what she was feeling.

"I don't hate my dad," she said, struggling through her tears, "I love him; I really love him. I don't want to hurt him; I just want him to stop putting me down. I want him to love me as his daughter."

As we talked, she told me of the devastation she felt when her father ignored her; then how the relationship worsened when she did some things (like drinking and drugs) to get his attention. She told of one day standing in front of him and screaming, "I'm your daughter, tell me you love me!" He pushed her aside and sat down to read the paper.

It is doubtful that Sally will ever completely recover from the emotional scars caused by this relationship. The tragedy is that Sally's story is being repeated again and again in families where parents don't understand the power of their words.

Despite the destructive potential of words, the

wonderful truth is that words can also heal. They can be like a soothing ointment and a ray of brilliant sunlight. They can console, calm, and comfort. They can bind up the brokenhearted and set the captive free.

Jesus used words that way. He described his words as having the power of life (John 6:63). He told his disciples to ingest his words as they were good food (6:51). Wherever he went he spoke words of comfort, cheer, and deliverance. "Just say the word," the centurion told Jesus, "and my servant will be healed" (Matt. 8:8).

Many times in relationships that is all it would take to bring healing and reconciliation—just a word. It might be "I love you" or "I'm sorry." Usually nothing eloquent or dramatic. The needed word at the right moment, expressed in love and understanding, can perform miracles. And to think, every one of us has access to that power! By using our tongue in the right way, we can change the world (beginning with our marriage and family) for the better.

Dale Carnegie wrote of his experience with the power of words. He went to the post office during the busy Christmas season to mail a package—in a hurry. To his dismay every window had a long line. As he waited impatiently, he noticed the people around him were in a bad mood. They were discourteous to one another. The clerks seemed harried and upset. He found himself caught up in the negative feelings.

Carnegie thought to himself: *I'm going to see what*

I can do to make a positive difference in this situation. He spoke calmly and kindly to the persons around him. They started responding in kind. The mood began to change across the entire post office. Occupied with his constructive behavior, Carnegie discovered the time passed quickly and he found himself at the window, facing a disgruntled clerk. What could he say to change the attitude of the clerk? Then he noticed the man had unusually beautiful hair.

"Sir, I could not help but notice your hair," said Carnegie. "I don't believe I have ever seen such a beautiful head of hair on a man."

The man took a step back and with both hands smoothed the sides of his hair. With a broad smile, he said, "Thank you. I have other people tell me that from time to time."

A pleasant conversation ensued while the clerk took care of the package. As he left, Carnegie observed the clerk's smile as he waited on the next customer. The atmosphere in the post office had changed. The power of a positive, truthful, healing word had touched and changed the lives of a number of people.

Words not only hurt or heal; they also instruct. Words are the vehicles by which truth is purveyed. In the beginning of time, God used words to explain his ways and to establish his relationship with man. By receiving and obeying the words of God, man is taught to live in this life and how to prepare for his eternal home.

As God uses words to instruct us and reveal himself to us, we use words to instruct our children and to give greater insight about ourselves to our mates and others.

As our children were growing up, Mary and I spent many hours with them simply giving words of instruction. Those occasions were not in a classroom setting and there were no formal exams, but learning was going on that would later be tested in the crucible of life. The classic Ephesian passage admonishes parents, "Fathers, do not exasperate your children; instead, bring them up in the training and instruction of the Lord" (6:4). *The Living Bible* translates the verse: "And now a word to you parents. Don't keep on scolding and nagging your children, making them angry and resentful. Rather, bring them up with the loving discipline the Lord himself approves, with suggestions and godly advice."

The first part of that verse, which talks about training, implies instruction (discipline) by example and attitude. The latter part focuses on the use of words (suggestions, advice). Children not only need example; they also need precept if they are to be properly nurtured and trained. We should not hesitate to give them simple, pure words of instruction.

I can remember spending many hours with my oldest son, Bob, in the rocking chairs on the front porch of our home, usually late at night. He would ask questions and I would try to give some answers. Often it seemed we were getting nowhere in those conversations. As Bob got older and finally was in college, he would tend to question my answers more. While we didn't always resolve the problem or agree on every point, a relationship was building and more learning was going on (in both of us) than either of us realized. I didn't understand at the time how precious those moments were.

Now Bob is married and has two children of his own. He told me recently, "Dad, those times we spent together on the front porch gave me understanding I never knew I had until the need arose in my own family." It takes time and effort to give words of instruction on a consistent basis to your children, but the rewards are incalculable.

If we are to minister to our mates and to the other people in our lives, we must consciously use words to edify, comfort, and enlighten. As our relationship with God cannot exist without God's speaking to us and our speaking to God, neither can human relationships survive without verbal interaction. Sometimes at the human level dialogue is avoided because it has become so painful. However, when we understand the power of words not only to hurt and heal, but also to instruct, we can employ the right words as instruments to alleviate or remove the pain.

In the case of difficulties between husband and wife, it is essential that one (preferably the husband) take the initiative to establish positive communication. That sounds simplistic, but if it is done according to the scriptural pattern, the results will be profound.

Relationships wither and die because of a lack of information passing between the persons involved. Let words be instructive by saying such things as, "I love you because . . . ," "I do care and I am going to demonstrate that by . . . ," "Tell me how you feel," "Let me tell you how I feel." A word of warning: When taking the initiative to give information to others, keep it positive. Avoid words of criticism or condemnation. There will be ample opportunity to work through areas of conflict when the relationship has become stronger. Many problems will solve themselves when positive dialogue is restored. Another important point: guard against becoming defensive and angry if the other person is critical or doesn't respond properly. Trust the power of truth through your words to do its work. "The Sovereign Lord has given me an instructed tongue, to know the word that sustains the weary. He wakens me morning by morning, wakens my ear to listen like one being taught" (Isa. 50:4).

THE CHOICE OF WORDS

Although sometimes we forget it or don't want to acknowledge it, the truth is we have control over the words we speak. Such control implies awesome responsibility. It is a serious matter when we understand our choice of words not only has far-reaching implications for the here and now, but will follow us to the judgment bar. "The good man brings good things out of the good stored up in him, and the evil man brings evil things out of the evil stored up in him. But I tell you that men will have to give account on the day of judgment for every careless word they have spoken. For by your words you will be acquitted, and by your words you will be condemned" (Matt. 12:35-37). With such a weighty accounting facing us, we would do well to look more closely at the process by which we choose our words.

The Bible puts it simply: "The heart of the righteous weighs its answers, but the mouth of the wicked gushes evil" (Prov. 15:28). This means we cannot afford to speak before we think. We not only reap eternal benefits, but we save many present heartaches if we think about what we are going to say before we say it.

What kind of thought process do we go through in order to make the right word choices? First of all, we have to consider what God has to say about the matter. In choosing our words we need to monitor a mental checklist of scriptural standards. Is what I am about to say truthful? Helpful? Kind and considerate? Critical? Self-serving? A good question to ask is, "What would Jesus say in this situation?"

Some matters should not be discussed until time is spent in prayer. How much more intelligently and objectively could we talk about some things if we had first presented them to the Lord? It stands to reason that a time of spiritual contemplation would give us a clearer mind, a broader perspective, and a better attitude about any subject we could name. How great it would be if when matters of disagreement arose with our spouse, our child, or our friend, we would say, "I'm not spiritually prepared to discuss this right now. How about looking at it again on Tuesday?" Sound impractical or superspiritual? In light of the track record some of us have in these situations, it might not hurt to consider a new approach.

In choosing our words, we also should take into account the effect on others of what we say. One of the biggest mistakes we make in our communication is our failure to consider how others are going to perceive what we say. We may feel very good about our words; our intentions and our motivation may be pure; but our message probably will be lost or misunderstood if we overlook this important factor. Jesus always based his words on the perception of the hearers. He spoke in language they could understand. He told stories with which they could identify. Often when he spoke it was as though he was seeing the world through their eyes. If we are to communicate properly, we must follow his example.

Another important consideration in our choice of words is how what we say will affect our image of ourselves and others. Since we are in control of our speech, the temptation is to make our words self-serving. As we have already seen, that is a mistake because in the end we fail to communicate the desired message. The image we have of ourselves is affected by what we hear ourselves say. While it is an undisputed fact that a strong self-image is necessary to positive relationships, we also understand that our self-image must be kept in proper balance. Therefore, we must choose words that correctly portray who we are and what we are. A general rule to remember is that people will base their image of us not on what we say we are, but what they perceive us to be in our relationship to them.

If we want to feel good about ourselves, we have to believe what we say. Truthfulness and integrity in our words are essential to a strong self-image. While it is possible for our consciences to be seared and for us to believe a lie (even about ourselves), when we are sensitive to the Holy Spirit, we will be checked any time our words do not reflect the truth or when they demonstrate a bad attitude. We understand that "from the overflow of the heart the mouth speaks" (Matt. 12:34). For our own sakes, we must choose our words carefully.

As Christians the image others have of us is extremely important. We are to be seen as light, salt, a city set on a hill. Our life is to be a fruitful vine, displaying love, joy, peace, patience, kindness, goodness, faithfulness, gentleness, and self-control (Gal. 5:23). When our words contradict this image, people are confused and disillusioned, especially those of our household. James spoke clearly to this problem: "With the tongue we praise our Lord and Father, and with it we curse men, who have been made in God's likeness. Out of the same mouth come praise and cursing. My brothers, this should not be" (3:9-10).

In our choice of words we must steer clear of any expressions that could be perceived as not characteristic of a true Christian.

A mother fell under conviction because of her habit of berating her nine-year-old son. Often she would lose her temper and say things to him she knew were deeply hurtful to his self-image and to her relationship with him. On her knees she made a vow to God that she would never say anything demeaning to him again. She had hardly finished her prayer when the front door opened and slammed shut, shaking the whole house. Billy was home from school. The mother felt a flood of anger sweep over her. "How many times have I told him not to slam that door?"

Billy came into the den where she was and, without a word, threw his lunch pail on the floor. Before she could respond to his seeming defiance, he ran down the hallway into his bedroom and deliberately slammed that door.

"I'm going to get that kid," she said. "He knows better than that." She rushed down the hallway, her temper raging, angry words ready to fly out of her mouth. As she put her hand on the bedroom door, the voice of God arrested her. "Didn't you just make a vow to me that you would never again verbally abuse your son?"

"Yes, Lord, but . . ."

"Then take your hand off that door, stand there for a moment, and let me give you strength." She felt her anger receding and a calmness flowing into her.

After a few minutes, she quietly opened the bedroom door. Billy was lying across his bed, face down, sobbing softly. She sat down beside him and rubbed his back. Finally he looked up and wiped the tears from his cheeks.

"What's the matter, son?" she gently asked.

"Mom, this has been the worst day of my life. My best friend told me he didn't like me anymore, and I flunked my math test."

On that day a mother and her son learned a lesson of life that would forever enhance their relationship. "The tongue has the power of life and death" (Prov. 18:21).

THE TIMING OF WORDS

The Bible makes quite an issue out of *when* to say what we say. It speaks of the goodness of a "timely" word (Prov. 15:23). One of the more famous Scriptures in the Old Testament eloquently describes a word fitly spoken: "A word aptly spoken is like apples of gold in settings of silver" (Prov. 25:11).

We have seen that a basic scriptural guideline for communication is that we should be slow to speak. In a later chapter we will return to this theme. Such an admonition, however, in no way negates the vital importance of our speaking the right words at the appropriate time.

The book of Ecclesiastes declares, "There is a time for everything, and a season for every activity under heaven" (3:1). Concerning one of those purposes, it says there is "a time to be silent and a time to speak" (3:7). As if to underscore the importance of timing, the book of Proverbs speaks in no uncertain terms about the man who doesn't understand this principle. "Do you see a man who speaks in haste? There is more hope for a fool than for him" (29:20). Strong language, but a crucial point.

The right words spoken at the wrong time can cause major problems. In the delicate matter of human communication, timing is all-important. Take for instance the positive, affectionate words of a husband to his wife when she is upset because he has not helped with the dishes. He would be better off to keep his mouth closed, demonstrate his love in some practical, helpful way, and save his words for a more appropriate time. Or the case of a mother who feels the need to talk to her teenage son about the providence of God when he has just been jilted by his girlfriend. Her well-intentioned words will probably be met with frustration, if not anger.

The foregoing examples point up the fact that timing should be determined by the needs of the person communicated with and not by the one doing the communicating. Positive communication depends upon being sensitive to the needs of others. As we think and pray about what we are to say and when we are to say it, we need to remember those golden apples in the silver bowl.

"He who guards his lips guards his life, but he who speaks rashly will come to ruin" (Prov. 13:3). It takes much thought and consideration to speak the language of love.

LANGUAGE LESSON

For use in individual study or family devotions

1. Recall two or three occasions when someone used language that injured you or someone you know.

2. Try to remember several occasions when someone used language that built up either you or someone you know.

3. Imagine the difference that could be made in each situation had the person heeded (or not heeded) the guideline *Think Before You Speak*.

Speak the Truth in Love

Speaking the truth in love, we will in all things grow up into him who is the Head, that is, Christ. . . . Therefore each of you must put off falsehood and speak truthfully to his neighbor, for we are all members of one body.

Ephesians 4:15, 25

Do not lie to each other, since you have taken off your old self with its practices.

Colossians 3:9

T H R E E
Speak the Truth in Love

It seems incongruous that the apostle Paul would write to the saints at Ephesus and tell them to "speak the truth" and to "put off falsehood," or that he would urge the "holy and faithful brothers" at Colossae to "not lie to each other." Since we know he was writing under the inspiration of the Holy Spirit, we cannot question the validity of his statements. We must take for granted that some of the Christians at Ephesus and Colossae were not always telling the truth. What was proper admonition for these two churches in Paul's day is appropriate for the church today.

Whether we like to admit it or not, Christians in the modern church have a problem with always telling the truth. It is not that we are consistently telling bald-faced lies or being dishonest. Our problem, as was no doubt the case in those early churches, is with exaggeration or what some might call "little white lies." Of course, we understand there is no such thing as a white lie. An untruth is an untruth as far as God is concerned. However, we are adept sometimes at putting tassels on the facts or we may tell the truth, but not the *whole* truth.

These problems with extending or shading the truth usually stem from our need to make a point—to make ourselves look good or someone else look bad. Whatever the reason, such practices mar our Christian testimony and present a major obstacle to proper communication.

THE POWER OF TRUTH

God says we must speak the truth in our communication with others for a good reason. Truthful words are the most powerful words we can use. We have the feeling sometimes that we must help the truth in order to make a case stronger or a point more emphatic. That is a fallacy. The moment we dilute, shade, or change the truth, we violate the Scripture and weaken our position. We need to learn to trust the truth, to have confidence in its power for good.

One of the most significant Scriptures in the entire Bible contains these words of Jesus: "You will know the truth, and the truth will set you free" (John 8:32). The reason people are bound by doubt, fear, prejudice, or any other negative force is because they don't know the truth. Most of the things that trouble us could be resolved immediately if we just knew the truth about these matters. Most of our childhood fears were swept away in the light of the knowledge we received as we grew older.

A primary objective in our communication with other people should be to impart truth, using honest, straightforward, unambiguous language. Our yes should mean yes and our no should mean no (Matt. 5:37; James 5:12). We should avoid beating around the bush. The apostle Paul asked the question, "If the trumpet does not sound a clear call, who will get ready for battle?" (1 Cor. 14:8).

Clarity and truthfulness are important in all our communication, but they have special significance when speaking with younger people. Children and young people have not yet learned to look for hidden meanings or to read between the lines. They respond most positively to the simple truth.

Mary and I have raised three children, two boys and a girl. At this writing our two sons are married (with children of their own). We learned a little bit about childrearing during those years. In fact, we might even qualify for some kind of special certificate since at one point all three children were teenagers at the same time. One of the things we tried to do from the beginning was to be absolutely honest with our children. We didn't perpetuate the Santa Claus, Easter Bunny, or Tooth Fairy myths. (Neither did we ridicule or poke fun at these stories.) Since they were preacher's kids, as they got older we didn't try to shield them from the realities of that life. When they asked, we told them the truth about church problems. When they complained about certain rules and areas of discipline, we did our best to explain the reasoning behind those things. Anytime they asked questions, we tried to take the time to give honest answers. Now, when I observe how they are functioning as mature Christian adults, I see that the truth we gave them then is still operating powerfully in their lives today.

When we are not open with one another in our communication, we set up destructive forces in our relationships. One of the primary ways we get to know one another is through the revelation of language. God, from the beginning, revealed himself to Adam and Eve by talking directly with them. When Adam and Eve broke communication with God through their disobedience and sin, God set the example of how to deal with broken relationships. He arbitrarily reached out to those who had hidden themselves from him. For their part, Adam and Eve, in answering for their deeds, were less than truthful. They shaded the truth and made excuses, trying to justify and protect themselves. Their untruthfulness only made matters worse, as it always does. They were the first to prove the validity of the poet's expression, "O what a tangled web we weave, when first we practice to deceive."

In a relationship, the harvest of misunderstanding and alienation is seeded by deceit and dishonesty. When we hide ourselves from one another, when we won't reveal our true feelings, when we send mixed messages, we are disobeying the command of God, and we are destroying the very foundation for a positive relationship. I have witnessed many times the devastating effects of untruthfulness.

Some time ago, a lady talked with me about seeking a divorce from her husband. The basis of her complaint was that her husband was thoughtless and uncaring. She told me a story to illustrate her point.

For several years she had been dropping hints to her husband about a certain set of china she had her heart set on. She got very angry at her husband because he never seemed to pick up on her clues. He knew she was upset, but when he would ask, she would not tell him why. Eventually, out of frustration, she decided if she were ever to own those dishes, she would have to buy them herself. She saved a few dollars from her grocery money each week until she finally had enough to purchase the set of china. All this was done without her husband's knowledge. Then she decided she would put him to the test.

Little did this unsuspecting husband know what lay in store for him when he came home from work late that afternoon. His wife had fixed a big meal, set the table with candles, and, of course, with her new china. The test was to see if he would recognize the dishes she had been giving hints about for years. Guess what! He flunked the test. He knew something was going on, but being the unobserving soul he was, he never noticed the dishes. A few minutes into the dinner his wife broke into tears, jumped up from the table, and ran into the bedroom. After much pleading and begging, she finally told him what the problem was.

"How can I live with someone as thoughtless as

he?" she asked. While I could not excuse the husband for his apparent inattentiveness to the needs of his wife, I felt compelled to ask her a question.

"Did you ever think of letting your husband in on your secret and allowing him to share your joy?" She had never considered that possibility. How paradoxical it is that we go to such lengths to keep others from finding out the truth we so desperately want them to know.

The power of truth to heal and strengthen relationships cannot be overestimated. Nothing is more nurturing to a relationship than a feeling of trust inspired by a record of honesty and openness in communication. When a husband knows his wife has no hidden agenda, when a son knows his father will tell him what he really thinks, when a member knows his pastor speaks the truth in love, then relationships can be built that will have positive ramifications from here through eternity.

THE REASON FOR TRUTH

In the verses quoted at the beginning of this chapter, Paul gave three reasons for speaking the truth: to demonstrate maturity, to promote unity, and to strengthen one's testimony.

The context of Ephesians 4:15 is filled with terms that call for Christian growth and maturity: "that the body of Christ may be built up" (4:12), "become mature" (4:13), "attaining to the whole measure of the fullness of Christ" (4:13). Notice the thrust of this whole passage:

Then we will no longer be infants, *tossed back and forth by the waves, and blown here and there by every wind of teaching and by the cunning and craftiness of men in their deceitful scheming. Instead, speaking the truth in love, we will in all things* grow up into him *who is the Head, that is, Christ. From him the whole body, joined and held together by every supporting ligament,* grows and builds itself up *in love, as each part does its work.* (Eph. 4:14-16, emphasis mine)

The plea to speak truthfully is predicated on the proposition that we are no longer children spiritually. Children are known for their penchant to fantasize and exaggerate.

I heard of a little boy who was given to exaggeration, and his mother was trying to break him of the habit. One day he came running in from school and excitedly told his mother that a lion had chased him all the way home.

"Now, Johnny, you know that was no lion; it was only the neighbor's dog down the street. I want you to go upstairs to your room and ask the Lord to forgive you." In a few minutes Johnny came down the stairs, looking satisfied.

"Did you speak to the Lord, as I told you, Son?" his mother asked.

"Yes, Mother," said Johnny, "but the Lord said it was OK because when he first saw that dog, he thought it was a lion too."

We may smile at that story, but if we are not careful, in our eagerness to make an impression or to defend our position, we may very well join Johnny's league. When we are backed into a corner because of a mistake, instead of taking it on the chin and admitting our error, we may sidestep the blow by making a lame excuse or shifting the blame. When we are criticized, we may lash back with an exaggerated accusation rather than listen and turn the other cheek. When we lose, we may become angry and make sarcastic remarks instead of graciously congratulating the winner. It takes maturity to admit a wrong, accept a criticism, or be a gracious loser; but that is what this scriptural passage is calling for.

Mature behavior is important because, as in each of the instances noted above, such childish, self-centered behavior of not speaking the truth in love damages relationships and brings reproach on the name of Christ. On the other hand, a mature response brings respect and reconciliation. It also brings honor and glory to God. Paul was saying, "Don't be children who lie and exaggerate, but be grown-ups who tell the truth."

Another important reason for speaking the truth in love is that it brings unity to the body. The theme of Ephesians is unity. That unity is based upon every member of the body using his particular position, vocation, or gifts to build up (edify) the other members. In our conversation we are to edify one another by putting off falsehood and speaking truthfully (4:25). We are not to let any unwholesome talk come out of our mouths, but only that which is helpful for building others up according to their needs (4:29). There should be no obscenity, foolish talk, or coarse joking (5:4). We are told to speak to one another with psalms, hymns, and spiritual songs (5:19). Paul ended the epistle with a request for prayer concerning his words: "Pray also for me, that whenever I open my mouth, words may be given me so that I will fearlessly make known the mystery of the gospel" (6:19).

When we think of bringing unity to the body through the power of truth, we should keep in mind that the unity of the entire body depends upon the proper functioning of each of the parts of the body. When I speak the truth, I feel good about myself. I have a unity and harmony in my spirit. In my marriage, I am to be one flesh with my wife. Such an unparalleled sense of unity is possible only if I am open and honest with her. My family should function as a unit, with a minimum of friction and conflict, a microcosm of the body of Christ. For that to happen, I must take the initiative to demonstrate truthfulness to every member of my family.

Unity, in any context, depends upon harmony, agreement, and concord. These elements presuppose the willingness of each diverse part to fit into the whole. It is not necessary for each part to lose its individual identity in order to become a part of the whole. But it is essential that each part be known, or allow itself to be known, so other parts may know how to fit with it.

There can be no true unity in a marriage, a family, or a church unless each member is willing to reveal himself—his feelings, likes, dislikes—truthfully to the other members. As long as individual members hide themselves from one another through independent action, behavioral facades, or untruthful conversation, there will be no unity. One of the requirements that God lays down for personal revival is that we do not hide ourselves from our own family members (Isa. 58:7).

Paul admonished the Christians in Colossae not to lie to each other (Col. 3:9). He gave as support for this admonition the fact that Christians have taken off the old self with its practices. In other words, if we are new creatures in Christ, we are not to lie anymore. Lying is not becoming to a Christian. It mars our Christian testimony.

One of the strongest arguments for speaking the truth in love is that people have a right to expect the truth from us if we are Christians. At the top, at least near the top, of any list of Christian characteristics is truthfulness. The assumption is that Christians don't lie. This Old Testament precept is strongly reaffirmed in the New Testament.

As is the case with other Christian attributes, truthfulness faces its greatest test in the arena of intimate relationships. It is in our marriage and our family where our behavior is most well-known and most closely scrutinized, as it should be. One of the great lies of Satan is that our public image is more important than our inner character. The Scripture declares, "There is nothing concealed that will not be disclosed, or hidden that will not be made known. What you have said in the dark will be heard in the daylight, and what you have whispered in the ear in the inner rooms will be proclaimed from the roofs" (Luke 12:2-3). Our practice of truthfulness should begin where it counts the most—in our own home, with our own family members. If anyone can testify to our openness, honesty, and integrity, it should be those closest to us.

Because truthfulness with our family members is so important, we must be alert to some areas of vulnerability in this regard. For instance, the way we treat certain people in public should square with the way we talk about them in private. There should not be a double standard—one public and one private. There is nothing wrong in sharing with family members, including older children, the truth about relationship problems or personality conflicts, as long as it is done discreetly and in love. Such a practice can be instructive if it is handled properly. However, the danger lies in saying one thing about a relationship to the family in private and then putting on an entirely different face in public. Kindness, consideration, and forbearance should be the standard privately and publicly.

Inconsistencies between public image and private character can be particularly disillusioning to children. While adults may see discrepancies as necessary for professional or social reasons and to be taken for granted in our society, children tend to view the matter in more simplistic terms — to them an untruth is an untruth, regardless of the reason.

I have talked with many children of professionals, particularly those whose parents were in the ministry or the military. With those kids who had problems, inevitably a common theme would emerge: they were hurt and angry because their parents, usually their father, put on one face in public but a different one at home. They saw that practice as being dishonest and untruthful, and generally they felt they were caught in the squeeze of that deception. When this situation occurred in a Christian family, the effects seemed even more devastating because the child tied his view of his parents to his view of God.

Nothing is more spiritually edifying than witnessing the positive effects of a life changed by Christ through the consistency of Christian behavior. To be the kind of light we should be, we must scrupulously guard our Christian behavior at all times. This is particularly important in the intimate atmosphere of our home. Our truthfulness and honesty must be practiced first of all with our family. As our mistakes are most glaringly evident to our mates and children, so with them will the consistency of our Christian testimony have its most powerful effect. "The tongue that brings healing is a tree of life, but a deceitful tongue crushes the spirit" (Prov. 15:4).

THE USE OF TRUTH

It is of special significance that Paul used the phrase "in love" in conjunction with speaking the truth. He was aware, as are we, that truth sometimes is used as a weapon. A person may state the facts but do it in a way and at a time that brings much hurt. If he is confronted with his action, he will defend himself by saying, "I was only telling the truth — just stating the facts." And he might add for good measure, "Sometimes the truth hurts."

Whenever the truth is used in this manner, the reason can usually be traced to a selfish motive. Rather than speaking the truth for the right reasons, the person wanted to make his point, defend his position, or put the other person down. The truth should be told, but it should be done at the right time, for the right reasons, and with the right attitude.

The use of tact is always needful, but it is especially necessary when speaking a truth that may strike a sensitive nerve in another. Marie Curling wrote of a loving use of tact:

> *Jamie was trying out for a part in the school play. His mother told me that he'd set his head on being in it, though she feared he'd not be chosen. On the day the parts were awarded, I went with her to collect him after school. Jamie rushed up, eyes shining with pride and excitement. Then he said . . . , "I've been chosen to clap and cheer."* (Guideposts, *September 1978*)

Credit Jamie's teacher with a masterstroke of tact. Even the most potentially hurtful piece of truth can be received positively if it is communicated with love and concern.

One of the nagging questions about telling the truth is just how honest one should be. We have all heard horror stories about some well-intentioned person who got dead honest with his wife and confessed his sexual escapades before their marriage, only to have his wife fly into a rage and file for divorce.

My first year in college I was assigned a roommate who was to test the depth of my sanctification. The college officials thought they were doing us a favor when they put Tom and me together because we were both from the same hometown — in fact, from the same church. Although Tom and I knew one another well, we were not close friends because there were obviously personality differences. Anytime we got a little too close there seemed to be a friction between us that threatened to become open confrontation. So when I found out we were rooming together, I was more than concerned.

Being newly called to the ministry and tending to overspiritualize things to some degree, I hit upon what I perceived to be the ideal biblical solution to our dilemma. We would sit down together and be absolutely truthful with each other. We would describe what we didn't like about one another and try to find solutions to those problems. Then we would shake hands and room together in harmony as two Christian young men should. I was happy with my idea, and when I told Tom, he seemed pleased too.

When the time for our discussion came, I graciously let Tom speak first. As he began to enumerate the things he didn't like about me, I felt my anger rising. He seemed to be arrogantly enjoying taking me apart. The only thing that saved me from "popping him one" was I knew my time was coming. However, as he continued to talk and I continued to get angrier, I knew this was an exercise in futility and frustration. Our attempt at honesty was blowing up in our faces. We never finished our talk. I moved out the next day.

When I look back on that episode with Tom, I realize that what I really wanted was the opportunity to tell him what I thought of him. Although it didn't turn out that way, I set the session up basically for my benefit. That was the mistake. Our judgment of when and how to use truth in sensitive situations must be guided by our concern for others. If the intent of our speaking is primarily to vent our own feelings or clear our conscience, we had better rethink whether we should speak at all. Our motivation for speaking the truth in these instances must be love, and love will do nothing that will hurt or destroy a relationship.

When relationships are as they should be, especially in the case of a husband and wife who are truly "one flesh," there can be no secrets. However, the dynamics and circumstances of each relationship are different. How and when certain truths are spoken must ultimately be left to the loving discretion of those involved. Speaking the truth is essential to speaking the language of love.

LANGUAGE LESSON

For use in individual study or family devotions

1. Think of one of the last experiences you had with trying to speak the truth in love. What did you do wrong? What did you do right? How could you have done better?

2. Try to recall one of the last times you were hurt by someone who failed to exercise the guideline explained in this chapter. What do you wish that person would have done? Are you satisfied with the way you responded? Why, or why not?

3. Think of someone who recently spoke the truth in love to you or someone you know. What can you learn from the way that person used this important language of love?

Disagree, but Don't Argue

Starting a quarrel is like breaching a dam; so drop the matter before a dispute breaks out.

Proverbs 17:14

Get rid of all bitterness, rage and anger, brawling and slander, along with every form of malice.

Ephesians 4:31

F O U R
Disagree, but Don't Argue

We come now to one of the most vital aspects of the communication process. Probably more relationships are ruined because of disagreements escalating into arguments than from any other cause. Nothing is more psychologically and spiritually devastating than a full-blown argument where tempers and language rage out of control. The Bible characterizes it as a dam breaking—a swift and sudden destructive force that leaves many casualties in its wake.

All of us have experienced the dam breaking and the sense of utter helplessness and hopelessness that follows. As we pick up the pieces, we vow it will never happen again. But inevitably the water rises again behind the dam and the stage is set for another confrontation, this one perhaps even more ruinous. It doesn't have to be that way. This chapter examines how strife develops and what steps can be taken to keep the dam from breaking.

THE INEVITABILITY OF DISAGREEMENT

I heard the story of an evangelist who went to a certain church for a revival and on the first night of the meeting, during his introductory remarks, told about his relationship with his wife. "In twenty-eight years of marriage," he said, "my wife and I have never had a disagreement." Upon hearing that statement one man in the congregation got up and left. A few weeks later a friend happened to see the man downtown and asked him why he left the revival on the first night and never came back. "You remember that evangelist talking about being married for twenty-eight years and never having a disagreement with his wife?" the man asked. "Well, I figured if he would lie about that, he would lie about anything." He could not conceive any relationship without some disagreements.

Our very nature sets each of us up to come at life differently. First of all, God created us as unique individuals. No two of us are completely alike, not even identical twins. Add to our individual differences the diversity of our cultural backgrounds and there is brought into play an array of possibilities for disagreement.

The differences in human beings make for the rich texture of our relational environment. We learn from and are enriched by those differences in others. In our more intimate relationships those differences bring out the best in us as we struggle to adjust and accommodate. However, it is the disagreements that stem from those differences that pose such a challenge.

In my many years of marital counseling, I have talked with quite a number of starry-eyed young people who knew they were ready for marriage. They thought they had discussed all there was to discuss and they had worked through any problems they could possibly face. Usually I could pose one question that would open up a whole new area of discussion. I would ask if they had decided what time they would go to bed at night or what time they planned to get up in the morning. Generally they would giggle a little bit, look at each other, and wind up saying it really wasn't that important. As far as they were concerned that was one of those matters that would take care of itself. However, when they were forced to discuss the question, they were often very surprised to find they had some very different ideas on the subject and perhaps even strong disagreement. Little did they realize that from such insignificant stuff divorces are made.

For the purpose of analyzing the anatomy of an argument, let's look a little more closely at this subject. Suppose this new husband is accustomed to staying up all hours of the night watching the late, late show. And suppose that his bride is one of these whose lights go out at 10 P.M. No problem the first few blissful weeks of marriage, but when the routine sets in, matters change. She begs him to come to bed, but he wants to see this particular show. He asks her to stay up, but she can't keep her eyes open. When he finally comes to bed, she has been asleep for a couple of hours, but he feels amorous. She doesn't want to wake up, and besides she is a little hurt because she had to go to bed alone, so she is resistant to his advances. Now he complains his needs are being ignored, and as he turns over, he makes a cutting remark about his wife's coldness.

Let's look at another couple's problem with the time to get up. Upon the return from the honeymoon, the husband gets up for work at 5:30 A.M. to a cold, dark house and an empty kitchen. All his life he was used to his mother being up before anyone else, and when he sat down for breakfast there were hot biscuits and about anything else his heart desired. As for his little wife, who is still snuggled in her bed, she has been used to getting her "beauty sleep" and, if she asked just right, her mommy would probably bring her breakfast in bed. Don't ask her to function at such an ungodly hour. She couldn't even find the Bisquick.

Of course, scenarios of this type are endless, but the point is that common differences can lead to disagreements that often turn into arguments. No relationship can survive a constant breaking of the dam. The biblical injunction is to stop the process of escalation before strife breaks out.

THE FALLACY OF ARGUMENT

The plea of the apostle Paul to the Christians of Ephesus was to stop their arguing. In clear language he said, "Stop being mean, bad-tempered and angry. Quarreling, harsh words, and dislike of others should have no place in your lives" (Eph. 4:31, TLB).

Arguing is a losing proposition. Someone has said there is no way to win an argument—even if you win, you lose. According to the book of Proverbs, quarreling and arguing are the province of fools. "A fool's lips bring him strife, and his mouth invites a beating" (18:6); "Every fool is quick to quarrel" (20:3); "A fool gives full vent to his anger, but a wise man keeps himself under control" (29:11).

If the Scripture teaches so strongly against this behavior, why do we persist in practicing it? I believe there are two basic reasons: first, we are not fully aware of just how destructive it is; and second, we don't know how to stop it.

Arguing is one of the most psychologically damaging of behaviors. It leaves the participants emotionally exhausted and mentally depressed. Using the analogy of the broken dam, when the flood tide has passed, there is little to do but survey the damage and make some attempt to pick up the pieces. In the aftermath of an argument, there is usually an exercise in mental gymnastics where we alternately berate ourselves and condemn the others involved. Seldom is an issue settled through argument, which means the problem still hangs over our heads, now heavier than ever. So we wind up depressed, our self-image eroded, our relationship strained or broken, and the problem bigger than ever.

The whole process has been counterproductive.

This kind of strife and contention also takes a heavy spiritual toll. Generally, in an argument, we have been unkind, even mean. Our Christian character has been questioned and our testimony harmed. We feel convicted, perhaps alienated from God, because of our behavior. We may have broken a vow to God or a promise made to loved ones. Spiritual recovery can take weeks or months.

As I write this description of the effects of an argument, my spirit rebels against it. I feel it in the pit of my stomach. I relive some personal experiences. I envision again traumatic scenes recounted by counselees. All of it makes me want to go back and remove or rewrite the last couple of pages. I look at the stack of resource books on my desk and they all have nice names with warm chapter titles. I wonder if anyone wants or needs to read about the damage caused by strife and contention. But in my heart I know we need to be reminded so we can gain new insight and receive spiritual strength to apply God's remedy to this painful problem. May we never again have our relationships devastated by the swirling waters of a broken dam!

THE STOPPING OF CONTENTION

Now we come to a vital truth — the extraordinarily simple solution for stopping strife before it breaks out. Probably written by Solomon some 3500 years ago, this admonition is just as relevant and valid today as it was then. Human nature hasn't changed and neither has God's law. "If you see the water trickling through the cracks in the dam," Solomon advised, "Drop the matter before the dispute breaks out" (Prov. 17:14); that is, before the dam breaks. What a simple, yet profound, solution!

What does it mean to "drop the matter?" The King James Version reads: "Leave off contention before it be meddled with." In other words, we are to stop discussing the matter—drop the subject for the time being. This is an emergency measure. If the dam is about to break, it is not very smart to pour more water behind the dam. But that is what we do. When tempers are flaring, voices are rising, and the subject is red hot, we plunge in where angels fear to tread. We are determined to make our point and to settle this problem, no matter what. Then we wonder why the dam breaks.

When the warning signs appear in a discussion, we recognize that we must back off. Someone has said, "Whether on the road or in a discussion, when you see red, stop." We might say (as kindly as possible), "I'm a little too upset to discuss this now; let's talk about it later." Or we might end the discussion without giving any particular reason. Just stop pursuing the subject we know is going to lead to disaster. This approach may not be well received by the other person involved, but we have to take that risk. The other person will soon get the idea because it is difficult to argue with oneself. That is a basic premise in this solution: It takes two to argue.

The idea is not to sweep the matter under the rug

but to give a little time for the water to recede behind the dam. Sometimes that takes only a few
minutes; in other cases it may take a few hours, a
few weeks, or months. It may mean coming back
to a subject several times and dropping it each time
the water begins to rise. In many cases even a few
minutes may make a big difference. It is amazing
how quickly feelings and perspectives change. A
matter that was volatile a short time before may even
become humorous when tempers have cooled.

Mary and I learned when our children were growing up that some subjects, if dealt with on the spot,
could quickly become potential argument starters.
We started putting those subjects on the agenda for
an upcoming family meeting. At a different time and
in a different setting (when there was less water behind the dam), we found these problems could be
settled quickly and with a minimum of fuss.

A few areas of disagreement exist in most relationships that may never be resolved. Anytime they
are discussed, a spark is ignited. It may be that a
compromise of "agreeing to disagree" will have to
be affected. However, even in these areas, effort
should continue to find solutions. Sometimes after
many years of disagreement, a new approach will
be discovered to an old problem and an understanding will be reached that was never thought possible.
That can be a most satisfying accomplishment.

Keep in mind that disagreement is not the problem. It is the bitterness and rage resulting from the
disagreement that does the damage and causes the

sin. There is no sin in disagreeing. Neither is there sin in anger, if it is properly directed. The tragedy of argument is the verbal (and sometimes physical) abuse that generally ensues from such an exchange. That is what the Bible says must not happen.

The wisdom of avoiding contention is commended again and again in the Scriptures. "A patient man has great understanding, but a quick-tempered man displays folly" (Prov. 14:29); "A man's wisdom gives him patience; it is to his glory to overlook an offense" (19:11); "It is to a man's honor to avoid strife, but every fool is quick to quarrel" (20:3); "The Lord's servant must not quarrel; instead, he must be kind to everyone, able to teach, not resentful" (2 Tim. 2:24). What God commands and commends, we cannot afford to ignore.

THE BALANCE OF ANGER

While the Bible condemns anger that results in wrath (rage, fury, vengeance), it does not indicate anger itself is a sin. In fact, anger is an attribute God possesses. "God is a righteous judge, a God who expresses his wrath every day" (Ps. 7:11). The history of Israel records many instances when the anger of God was kindled against that nation for its disobedience. Since we are made in the image of God, we can say that God created us with the ability to get angry. An admonition in the New Testament settles the question of whether it is possible to be angry and yet not sin. "In your anger do not sin: Do not let the sun go down while you are still angry" (Eph. 4:26).

Sin occurs when anger is not controlled. There are two major areas in which the Christian must control his anger: direction and duration. Our anger should not be directed toward individuals (Matt. 5:22). We should rather focus our indignation on certain principles, practices, or processes. When we personalize our anger, we are in danger of violating the rights of others and displaying characteristics which are not becoming to a Christian. While it may seem unrealistic or impractical not to personalize anger, it is a well-known principle of human interaction that to direct anger at another is counterproductive. Personalized anger creates obstacles that may eliminate the possibility of conflict resolution.

The direction of anger should also be controlled as to the manner in which it is expressed. When anger is vented as rage, fury, vengeance, bitterness, hatred, judgment, or condemnation, it becomes sin. If anger results in a tirade, vulgar language, or physical abuse, it has gotten out of control and must be repented of. This is not to imply that feelings of anger should be repressed or ignored. There is good evidence that such a practice is harmful—physically, psychologically, and spiritually—and usually results in the anger manifesting itself in other destructive ways. A good practice is to express the anger to a trusted friend—a third, uninvolved party. Or find some physical outlet for the feelings of anger—jogging, tennis, racquetball, perhaps punching a bag. It is always appropriate to take our anger to the

Lord. Not only can he calm an angry spirit, but he can show us where we might be wrong in our feelings or he can help us to properly channel these feelings.

God also expects us to control our anger with regard to duration. He tells us not to let it last beyond sundown. In other words, get over it quickly. One way to control the duration of our anger is to express it, defuse it, get it out in some positive way. Another method of control is to stop mulling it over. The passage of time has a way of dissipating the intensity of the anger. If we do not keep stoking the fire, it will eventually cool down.

One more important, positive thought about anger: If it is expressed within the scriptural guidelines noted above, it can be a healthy experience. Martin Luther said, "When I am angry I can write, pray, and preach well, for my whole temperament is quickened, my understanding sharpened, and all the mundane vexation and temptations depart." Since getting angry is part of our makeup as human beings, we cannot avoid periodic confrontations with those we love. If we will keep in mind the pitfalls involved, those confrontations can be a creative, therapeutic force in our relationship.

In his book, *The Friendship Factor,* Alan McGinnis lists five techniques for use in a "clean confrontation" or a "Christian fight":

1. Talk about your feelings, not your friend's faults.
2. Stick to one topic.
3. Allow your friend to respond.

4. Aim for ventilation, not conquest.
5. Balance criticism with lots of affection.

When properly controlled, the strong emotions discussed in this chapter can powerfully speak the language of love.

LANGUAGE LESSON

For use in individual study or family devotions

1. When was the last time *you* were involved in an unpleasant argument? From the list given near the end of this chapter, drawn from Alan McGinnis's book, which of the five techniques were violated in the disagreement? What could have been said or done that would have changed the argument into a reasonable disagreement?

2. Sometimes when we don't agree with another person, it is better to remain silent. At other times, it is better to openly disagree. Make a list of possible occasions when it is better to disagree with someone than to agree. Also, make a list of occasions common to your family life when it is better to remain quiet.

3. From your knowledge of the Scriptures, think of occasions when disagreements took place and analyze how well or how poorly the people involved handled the problem.

Love

Control Your Response

A *gentle answer turns away wrath, but a harsh word stirs up anger.*

Proverbs 15:1

And *the Lord's servant must not quarrel; instead, he must be kind to everyone, able to teach, not resentful. Those who oppose him he must gently instruct.*

2 Timothy 2:24-25

F I V E
Control Your Response

As a young pastor, I was called to the home of a couple that was having severe marital problems. I was told that they argued incessantly and that often their behavior toward one another turned violent. In my inexperience I decided the best way to resolve the problem was to get the whole family together for a full airing of their disagreements.

The husband, wife, their three daughters, and I sat in the living room of their beautiful home and began what was to be a near-tragic learning experience for all of us. Shortly into the discussion it became evident that the lines of battle were clearly drawn — the wife and daughters on one side and the husband on the other. The wife began to make angry accusations against her husband, and these were loudly attested to by each of the daughters. The tension in the room became intense. I knew an explosion was about to take place, but I felt helpless to prevent it.

Suddenly the man jumped to his feet, picked up a footstool, raised it over his head toward his wife and shouted at her: "I'll break every bone in your body!" The girls screamed and ran from the room as I tried to wrestle the piece of furniture from the exasperated husband. He dropped the footstool and rushed out the door to the garage. "He's going to get his shotgun," his wife exclaimed frantically. Needless to say, one frightened young pastor prayed fervently for divine intervention.

Fortunately for all of us, the husband did not get his gun but instead went out a side door and took a walk around the block. Later I was able to calm the situation down and bring about the semblance of a reconciliation. However, the principle I saw so graphically demonstrated that day taught me a lesson I would never forget.

That couple (both Christians, by the way) seemingly had no insight into what they were doing to each other. Each was so intent on making his or her point that they totally lost sight of the cause-and-effect relationship of their behavior. Their harsh words toward one another had a singular effect: they stirred up their anger. They had to learn how to stop that approach to their problems before any solid progress could be made toward reconciliation.

The Bible is filled with examples of cause-and-effect relationships: what we sow, we will reap; if we call, he will answer; if we seek, we will find. One of the most practical and relevant of these reciprocal principles is stated in the proverb: "A gentle answer turns away wrath, but a harsh word stirs up anger" (Prov. 15:1). We instinctively know how true that principle is, yet we consistently violate it in our interpersonal communication.

This scriptural truth teaches that we should consciously avoid harshness in our language when responding to others. We should lower our voice, speak more slowly, and avoid threatening gestures. We should be kind, courteous, and "gently instruct" those who oppose us. Such behavior entails strong motivation and obvious control. That is where the problem lies.

THE CONCEPT OF CONTROL

It is difficult for us, especially those of us of the evangelical persuasion, to recognize that we exercise as much control over our behavior as we actually do. We tend to blame a lot of things on the "spirit" or on the devil that, in truth, we are responsible for. We find it easy to attribute our nonproductive (or even sinful) behavior patterns to personality, parents, or certain environmental circumstances.

The Bible clearly teaches the vital importance of the will in determining human behavior patterns. The whole theological concept of judgment is premised on the possibility of choice. God could not judge us on matters over which we have no control. The fact is we do have a choice; we can exercise our will to determine what our behavior will be.

Beginning with our decision to love God, through our decision to repent ("turn around"), and on to the day-to-day decisions to follow the commands of God, we demonstrate our control over the direction of our life. This process, of course, must filter down to the most intimate aspects of our relationships to others. It must guide the details of our behavior, which the Scripture reminds us are being divinely recorded to be revealed at the Day of Judgment: "For we must all appear before the judgment seat of Christ, that each one may receive what is due him for the things done while in the body, whether good or bad" (2 Cor. 5:10).

While we must take responsibility for our behavior, we also must understand it is not possible for us to make the right choices on our own. We must have God's help. We have countless examples in the Bible, beginning with Adam and Eve, which demonstrate the fallacy of making decisions without divine strength and wisdom. With God's help we will not fail; we will make the right behavioral choices. "I can do everything through him who gives me strength" (Phil. 4:13). When we love the Lord with all our heart, soul, and mind, we *will* be able to love our neighbors as ourselves.

If we have control over our behavior, how do we practically go about giving the proper response to others? The Scripture talks about a "soft" or "gentle" answer. Such a response obviously would involve language, tone of voice, gestures, and attitude.

The word content of our response determines to

a great degree how it is received by the other person. We will discuss "angry words" in a later section, but suffice it to say a soft answer would not contain harsh, critical, or judgmental words. The Bible encourages us to use "pleasant" words in our conversation. "Pleasant words promote instruction" (Prov. 16:21). "Pleasant words are a honeycomb, sweet to the soul and healing to the bones" (Prov. 16:24). The dictionary defines *pleasant* as "pleasing, agreeable, enjoyable." The most sensitive and difficult of subjects can be made much more palatable through the use of pleasant words. If our object is to communicate clearly certain facts and to avoid stirring up anger, it is logical for us to choose our words carefully.

Studies have indicated that tone of voice may be more important than any other element in our response. A loud, strident tone can mask the meaning of a positive message. On the other hand, a softer, kind voice can help even negative words to be received more amicably. The focus on tone of voice is aptly illustrated in this paradoxical statement supposedly made by a wife to her husband in the midst of a heated discussion: "You're speaking so loudly I can't hear a word you're saying." We sometimes get the idea the louder we speak the better our message is communicated. Usually the only message received in that situation is "I am very angry with you."

Again in the book of Proverbs, the Holy Spirit speaks so profoundly, yet practically, to this issue:

"A fool's lips bring him strife, and his mouth invites a beating" (18:6). If we want to avoid stirring up strife or inviting a beating (verbal and physical), we must consciously moderate the tone of our voice.

Another important aspect of control in communication is how we use gestures — such as our countenance, body posture, and hand movement. The softness and gentleness of our response can be significantly enhanced by an animated smile, an approving nod, or an extended hand. Jesus frequently touched people when he spoke with them. On one occasion he gathered a child in his arms to illustrate a point. Remember, those we speak with are *watching* what we *do* as well as *listening* to what we *say.* We should not be mechanical in our movements or our expressions, but should be aware constantly of the powerful communicative effect of our gestures.

Perhaps as critical as any other factor in the process of communication is the attitude of the communicator. Again, the vital element of control comes into play. It is said of a famous opera star that before she went on stage she repeated to herself, "I love my audience, I love my audience." This was not a gimmick or a play on words, but a conscious way of reminding herself that the people in the audience were her fans and friends. They paid their money to hear her perform. They were the reason for her success. When she remembered these things, it was not difficult to walk on stage with a loving feeling in her heart. And what a difference it made in her performance!

In our response to others, we would do well always to check our attitudes. With family members we need to remind ourselves of our love for them. We need to be sensitive to what may be going on with them at the moment. I have found it helpful when talking with someone, especially if the subject matter is sensitive or the person is upset, to keep a silent prayer in my heart saying, "Lord, please help me really to know this person and give me the words to say that will be meaningful." It is surprising how that kind of spiritual attitude can affect in a positive way all aspects of our response.

Sometimes we will blame a poor job of communicating on our unique personality or our state of mind at the time. It is just our nature to be outspoken or reticent, we say. Or, we were tired, upset, or distracted. When we understand the broad spiritual and psychological implications of our responses and their impact, we cannot afford to make excuses. We must face the fact that we are in control of every verbal and nonverbal aspect of our communication — an awesome responsibility, but also an unbelievable privilege.

THE FOOLISHNESS OF ANGRY WORDS

A sage once said, "He who has a sharp tongue soon cuts his own throat." We have seen the truth of that statement demonstrated again and again. The losing of our temper, coupled with angry words, is as destructive a force as there is in the world.

The Bible has a lot to say about hot heads and loose

tongues. Listen to these observations recorded in the book of Proverbs: "A fool is hotheaded and reckless. A quick-tempered man does foolish things" (14:16-17). "A fool gives full vent to his anger. . . . An angry man stirs up dissension, and a hot-tempered one commits many sins" (29:11, 22). Hear the admonition of James: "So . . . the tongue is a small thing, but what enormous damage it can do. A great forest can be set on fire by one tiny spark. And the tongue is a flame of fire. It is full of wickedness, and poisons every part of the body. And the tongue is set on fire by hell itself, and can turn our whole lives into a blazing flame of destruction and disaster" (3:5-6, TLB).

Anger is what sets the tongue on fire, and it is the fiery tongue that "stirs up strife" and causes such enormous damage. In an earlier chapter anger was briefly discussed. At this point it would be helpful to look more closely at the process that culminates in angry words.

Being angry is not a sin, as we have already seen. What that anger leads to is the problem. Anger expressed verbally usually winds up in one of the following ways: (1) *outbursts* — lashing out, often in a loud voice; (2) *vengeance* — expressing bitterness, hatred, revenge, and an attitude of judgment; (3) *verbal abuse* — ventilating verbally, after zeroing in on a specific person with a specific accusation. When anger takes these forms it becomes sinful and is condemned in the Scriptures.

Anger can and must be controlled. In his book

Christian Counseling, Gary Collins, a well-known counselor, suggests four ways to gain greater control over anger:

Slowing One's Reactions

The old idea of counting to ten before speaking sometimes helps one to gain control before reacting in rage. Others have suggested the value of speaking slowly, not raising one's voice, pausing periodically (if possible), flexing the muscles (so they can relax), and mentally telling oneself to relax.

Dealing with Feelings of Inferiority

Hostility and anger often indicate that a person feels inferior, insecure, and lacking in self-esteem or self-confidence. If someone is made to feel inferior, he or she often reacts with anger in an attempt to assert his or her superiority. This is seen in arguments which frequently consist of two people trying to bolster themselves and each trying to make the other feel inferior. As a result there is anger and sometimes a loss of self-control.

Avoiding an Angry Mind-set

Some people look for the worst in almost every situation. They are perpetually critical, always negative, and invariably hostile. Most people find themselves slipping periodically into a negative mind-set, and unless this is resisted, we get caught in what has been called a "hos-

tility trap." The Scriptures instruct us to think about things which are right, pure, good and praiseworthy. Surely it is impossible to think such thoughts repeatedly and, at the same time, to wallow in anger, bitterness and hostility. The apostle Paul had a positive mind-set and an attitude of thanksgiving and praise to God. As a result he avoided anger, even when circumstances were difficult.

Growing Spiritually
Self-control is not something which must be done completely on our own. Self-control is listed in Galatians 5 as a fruit of the Spirit. Believers who sincerely desire to be led by the Holy Spirit will discover a slow decline in strife, jealousy, outbursts of anger, disputes and other "deeds of the flesh." With God's help we can learn love, patience, gentleness and self-control.

It is important to understand that when we speak of controlling anger, we are not implying it should be repressed. Such a practice is not helpful to relationships or healthful to the individual. The thrust of the biblical passages concerning dealing with anger is to recognize it for what it is and then to guide its direction and limit its duration. Secular theorists tend to encourage handling anger in one particular way—"express it, don't repress it." This has led to various (sometimes bizarre) suggestions as to how anger should be expressed. Walking, jogging, breaking dishes, and "scream" therapy are some of the methods suggested for "clearing the air" or venting hostility. Some research has indicated that such approaches tend to *increase* anger rather than *decrease* it.

The Christian does not have to accept the "express-repress" choice. He has the scriptural alternative to neutralize anger by recognizing its source and practicing humility, confession, and forgiveness. A common source of prolonged anger is the practice of "mulling over" or ruminating. Here the Christian has the perfect solution in Paul's admonition to think of the things that are true, noble, right, pure, lovely, admirable, and praiseworthy (Phil. 4:8). Anger handled according to the scriptural guidelines will not express itself in outbursts, vengeance, or verbal abuse.

Most of us are not given to frequent angry tirades that so grossly violate the biblical imperatives, but we do have consistent trouble with the day-to-day encounters where we ignore or overlook what we might term "smaller" violations.

A couple of years ago my daughter, Lorri, who was then nineteen, came into the office where I was working to ask me a question. I remember being somewhat frustrated and upset with the work I was doing and not in any particular mood to be interrupted. I answered her question as best I could and she left the room. A few minutes later she stuck her head back in the door.

"Are you mad at me about something, Dad?" she asked. I assured her I wasn't. "Well, you sure acted like it when you answered my question a few minutes ago."

I apologized and then pondered why she would think such a thing. Surely, after nineteen years she knew I loved her and wouldn't do anything to hurt her. In my mind I recounted my response to her. As I thought about it, I recalled the sense of irritation, even anger, that I felt when she interrupted my work. My words were short, hurried, without a hint of love and warmth. Probably I didn't smile or even act friendly. No wonder she thought I was angry. But the thing that bothered me most was she thought I was angry at *her.* Needless to say, that little episode has helped me to be more alert as to how I come across to others.

"A man of knowledge uses words with restraint, and a man of understanding is even-tempered" (Prov. 17:27).

THE FRUIT OF GENTLENESS

It is the *gentle* answer that turns away wrath. *Gentleness.* Just the sound of the word brings a good feeling. Listen to these positive definitions of "gentle": polite; courteous; generous; kind; serene; patient; not violent, harsh, or rough. Think about how these terms apply to our verbal responses.

Jesus used this term to describe himself: "Come to me, all you who are weary and burdened, and I will give you rest. Take my yoke upon you and learn from me, for I am *gentle* and humble in heart, and you will find rest for your souls" (Matt. 11:28-29). The *New American Standard Bible* renders the third beatitude of the Sermon on the Mount: "Blessed are the *gentle,* for they shall inherit the earth" (Matt. 5:5). Also, gentleness is listed as one of the fruits of the Spirit (Gal. 5:22-23).

Lest we get the impression that being gentle means being weak or suppressing our feelings or simply not telling it like it is, note the illustrative examples given by Charles Swindoll in his book, *Improving Your Serve:*

> *A wild stallion that has been tamed, brought under control, is described as being "gentle."*
> *Carefully chosen words that soothe strong emotions are referred to as "gentle" words.*
> *Ointment that takes the fever and sting out of a wound is called "gentle."*
> *In one of Plato's works, a child asked the physician to be tender as he treated him. The child used this term "gentle."*
> *Those who are polite, who have tact and are courteous and who treat others with dignity and respect are called "gentle" people.*

If you doubt the power of gentleness, think about this Scripture: "Through patience a ruler can be persuaded, and a gentle tongue can break a bone" (Prov. 25:15). *The Amplified Bible* puts it like this: "By long forbearing and calmness of spirit a judge or ruler is persuaded, and soft speech breaks down the most bonelike resistance."

We are so much more effective in our communication when we follow the scriptural pattern! A response that is controlled to be gentle through language, tone of voice, gestures, and attitude will not only eloquently speak the language of love, but will so much more adequately accomplish its intended purpose.

LANGUAGE LESSON

For use in individual study or family devotions

1. Try to recall at least two or three recent occasions when you realized *you* were failing to control your responses.

2. Ask yourself, and perhaps share with someone else, why on those occasions you said or did things you shouldn't have.

3. Try to think of ways you could have responded to demonstrate the language of love in show during those occasions.

4. Try to imagine how the other person would have responded to you if you had shown more gentleness and control.

Love

Confess Your Faults

Therefore confess your sins to each other and pray for each other so that you may be healed. The prayer of a righteous man is powerful and effective.

James 5:16

If we claim to be without sin, we deceive ourselves and the truth is not in us. If we confess our sins, he is faithful and just and will forgive us our sins and purify us from all unrighteousness.

1 John 1:8-9

S I X
Confess Your Faults

Admitting we are wrong when we make mistakes, acknowledging faults, confessing sins — these are some of the most difficult tasks a human being is ever called upon to do. Yet the rewards of such actions are incalculable. They not only vitally affect our relationships in the "here and now," but they actually determine our eternal destiny.

Several years ago, a couple on the verge of divorce came to me for counseling. They were well known in the community — multimillionaires, high on the social register. The last of their three daughters had gotten married just a few weeks before and so, when the wife filed for divorce, everyone was shocked.

When they came into my office, the husband sat on one side of the room and the wife on the other — physically separated as much as possible in that small space. The husband stated that he did not want a divorce and was puzzled at his wife's action. When I questioned the wife as to her reasons, she spoke softly, but straightforwardly.

"I don't believe in divorce," she said, "but I have decided I would rather live alone for the few years I have left than continue to live with a man who has treated me and our girls so badly for twenty-eight years."

She then proceeded to tell me how authoritarian, dogmatic, and mean her husband had been. She said that in their years of marriage he had hurt her and the children many times but not once in all those years had he apologized.

I asked the husband if he had done anything to his wife and family during those twenty-eight years for which he was sorry.

"Oh, many things."

"Did you apologize for any of those things?"

"I guess I didn't. She says I didn't and she's a good woman. She wouldn't lie."

I pushed the point further. "If it would save your marriage, would you be willing to tell your wife you are sorry for all those things?"

"You mean right now?"

"I don't know any better time."

He bowed his head a few seconds, then looked at his wife and said very deliberately, "OK, I really am sorry!"

When he said that, she jumped out of her chair, ran across the room, fell at his feet, and threw her arms around his legs. She buried her face between his knees and wept convulsively. Finally, she looked up at him, wiped the tears from her eyes, and said with a smile, "Now I know you really care!"

The next week they returned for another counseling session. They came hand-in-hand, smiling broadly.

"How have things been going?" I asked.

"Fantastic!" he responded. "It's been like a second honeymoon all week," she said. They both stated that they had never been so happy. The husband volunteered his appraisal of the situation. "It's a miracle," he said. "I apologize twenty-five times a day now. It really works!"

I saw them several times after that. The healing of their relationship was evident, but their joy in each other was something to behold. A husband's simple act of confession, coupled with the forgiveness of his wife, had turned years of hostility and bitterness into a new life of unbounded happiness.

Admitting faults is difficult, especially for men in our society. To some men, an admission of wrong is a sign of weakness. The Bible indicates just the opposite. As the priest of his household, a man is to set the example in repentance as well as reconciliation.

THE NECESSITY OF CONFESSION

Simply defined, confession in this context is the acknowledgment or admission of a wrong. It is a powerful act of the human will that prepares the way for repentance. To obtain forgiveness we are told we must first confess our sin and then forsake it (Prov. 28:13). Repentance and subsequent positive change are impossible without the initial step of confession.

An unwillingness to admit wrong is at the heart of most relationship problems. Instead of taking responsibility for our mistakes and sins, we become defensive and begin pointing the finger at others, placing the blame on them. Adam set that pattern in the beginning. When God asked him if he had eaten of the forbidden fruit, he said, "Yes, but . . ." He blamed his sin on "the *woman you* gave me." Not only did he imply Eve was the guilty party, but he also implicated God because God had given him the woman. How like Adam we are!

I taught high school for a few years while I was preparing for the ministry. One of my responsibilities was to supervise the intramural sports program. One day, during the softball season, a student came into my office and told me some of the players were having an argument with a passing motorist.

When I got to the scene, a group of the boys were jeering and taunting a very angry middle-aged man. A stray softball had hit his car while he was driving by the playground. He pointed to a dent in his fender he said was caused by the ball. Some of the boys made fun of his accusation and suggested he was trying to get a previously damaged fender fixed at their expense. I arrived just in time to take the brunt of a string of curse words from the man and an adamant promise to sue the school.

The unwillingness of any of the boys to admit their

wrong so enraged this man he was willing to go to almost any length to prove his point. I immediately apologized to the man and asked the team captain to do the same. I told him we were wrong for not doing a better job of protecting passing cars and we would pay for any damage to his car.

The change in the man's attitude was amazing. He allowed that "boys will be boys" and perhaps the dent in his fender had been there before. In any case he didn't want us to worry about the matter. The boys listened in disbelief. As the man drove off, we had the ideal opportunity to discuss the scriptural truth of admitting wrongs.

Often we bring disaster upon our head because we will not follow this principle. When we try to cover our sins, we reap the adverse results of our disobedience: (1) we will not prosper, (2) we will receive no mercy, and (3) we will create anger and disillusionment in others. On the other hand, when we are willing to confess and forsake our sin: (1) we will find good success, (2) we will obtain forgiveness, and (3) our relationships will be healed. "A man who refuses to admit his mistakes can never be successful. But if he confesses and forsakes them, he gets another chance" (Prov. 28:13, TLB). "Admit your faults to one another and pray for each other so that you may be healed" (James 5:16, TLB).

In a conflict situation, the simple admission "I was wrong" and a straightforward apology will literally work wonders. Many times we are hindered in making such a statement because we feel the other person is unwilling to do the same. We must understand that someone has to take the initiative. That is what the *agape* form of love is all about. It initiates positive action, regardless of the actions or attitudes of others. Usually, when a confession or apology is made, it elicits a similar response in the other person.

We may hesitate to apologize or admit we are wrong because we sincerely believe it is not our place. If there is a conflict, usually there is some wrong on both sides. We can always make right our part of the wrong. That is all God requires.

Confession draws us closer to God and to others. It is an irreplaceable part of the language of love.

THE PRAYER OF RECONCILIATION

Admitting we are wrong puts us in a position to pray for one another with an openness and sincerity not otherwise possible. In a relationship where there are unconfessed wrongs, prayer (if it is practiced at all) tends to be stifled, and even hypocritical. According to the Scripture, unresolved conflicts in relationships block worship and hinder answers to prayers (Matt. 5:23-24; 1 Pet. 3:7).

Perhaps the most basic of all theological principles is that our love for God is validated by our love for others (John 13:35; 1 John 4:20-21). When conflicts arise, we must make every effort to bring about a reconciliation; otherwise our love for God is in question. Prayer is one of the most effective tools we have to mend broken relationships.

When the straight-line method (person to person)

of communication fails, try the triangle method (person to God to person). Intercessory prayer works—especially in conflict situations. When we can't talk to the other person (for whatever reason), we can talk to God about the other person. That prayer should not be just a perfunctory prayer for the other person but a talking to God about the relationship. We should confess to God the ways in which we have failed in the relationship. (It is also best to confess to God before we confess to others.) We should ask God to give us discernment to know the other person after the Spirit, rather than after the flesh (2 Cor. 5:16) and pray for the right words to say when we do speak.

As we pray persistently and consistently for that person, our attitude will begin to change. We will become less self-centered, less concerned about our rights, and more concerned about our responsibilities. Our defenses will begin to crumble and we will see that person more objectively. In short, we will be much better prepared to effect a reconciliation.

Our prayer for a relationship also will have a spiritual impact on the other person. We can depend upon the Holy Spirit to touch that person in a way we never could. Our prayer will begin to draw us closer and closer together. That is using the language of love, through the Lord, to the other person.

The prayer of reconciliation can be prayed *with* another, as well as *for* another. As awkward as it may seem at first, a prayer with someone with whom we are having relationship difficulties will soon become quite natural. It is difficult to keep up a facade or maintain angry feelings when we are talking to the Lord together.

Let me make a few suggestions concerning praying with a person in a conflict situation. Your prayer doesn't have to be long, and it ought not be formal. If appropriate, hold hands or touch the other person's shoulder. Speak about your mutual needs, but don't hesitate to pray for yourself as it relates in a positive way to the other person.

In the book of Philippians Paul wrote a lot about relationships. When he came to the close of his letter, that theme was still on his mind as he admonished two distinguished ladies in the church to be reconciled to one another (4:2-3). In the following verses he seemed to speak to the anxiety that is caused by broken relationships, and he offered prayer as the remedy: "Let your gentleness be evident to all. The Lord is near. Do not be anxious about anything, but in everything, by prayer and petition, with thanksgiving, present your requests to God. And the peace of God, which transcends all understanding, will guard your hearts and your minds in Christ Jesus" (4:5-7).

Mary Carolyn Davies captures the spirit of the prayer of reconciliation in her poem, "A Prayer for Every Day."

> *Make me too brave to lie or be unkind.*
> *Make me too understanding, too, to mind*

The little hurts companions give, and friends,
The careless hurts that no one quite intends.
Make me too thoughtful to hurt others so.
Help me to know
The inmost hearts of those for whom I care
Their secret wishes, all the loads they bear,
That I may add my courage to their own.
May I make lonely folks feel less alone.
And happy ones a little happier yet.
May I forget
What ought to be forgotten; and recall
Unfailing, all
That ought to be recalled, each kindly thing,
Forgetting what might sting.
To all upon my way,
Day after day,
Let me be joy, be hope! Let my life sing!

We need to be reminded of the latter part of our first theme Scripture: "The prayer of a righteous man is powerful and effective" (James 5:16).

THE HEALING OF RELATIONSHIPS

According to God's formula, confession plus prayer equals healing. Leave out any part of that equation and it won't work. However, the end result (healing) is what we are after. In fact, that is what God has been about from the beginning — redemption, deliverance, and healing. That is why Jesus Christ came into the world. The final matter on God's agenda is the ultimate redemption and healing of his people — when his mortal children will put on immortality.

Right now, on the horizontal plane, God is concerned about how we treat one another. He makes our relationship to others a test of our love for him. At the final judgment, those who are told to depart from his presence are those who have failed to demonstrate their love and concern for others (Matt. 25:41-46).

This matter of our relationship with others is so important that God places it above our formal acts of worship: "But I tell you that anyone who is angry with his brother will be subject to judgment. . . . Therefore, if you are offering your gift at the altar and there remember that your brother has something against you, leave your gift there in front of the altar. First go and be reconciled to your brother; then come and offer your gift" (Matt. 5:22-24).

Some time ago I spoke with a pastor who was concerned because his church clerk had resigned — publicly, on a Sunday morning, and without informing the pastor ahead of time. In his remarks the clerk mentioned that he did not agree with the pastor in some areas, so he felt it would be better if he stepped down. The clerk did not return for Sunday evening worship. Several members of his large family walked out of the evening service before the message. That was Sunday; the pastor called me the following Tuesday. My first question was, "Have you talked to the clerk since he resigned?" His incredible answer:

"No, I haven't gotten around to that." His primary purpose in calling me, as a denominational executive, was to inquire about the procedure for selecting a new clerk.

The more I found out about this incident, the more unbelievable the pastor's behavior became to me. This clerk had been faithful to his responsibilities for years and had never caused a problem. He was related to a number of people in the church. The pastor had heard rumblings that some of these family members were hurt. Yet he had not had time to visit his former clerk.

This was a situation that called for the man of God to leave his gift at the altar and be reconciled to his brother. If full reconciliation was not possible, at least an effort should have been made to listen to his complaints, to clarify any points, and to offer an apology, if necessary. When the clerk did not come to him, it was the pastor's responsibility to initiate the reconciliation process. It is noteworthy that the foregoing Scripture states we are to leave our gift at the altar when we remember our brother has something *against us* — not when we remember we have something against our brother. (Of course, it is also necessary to be reconciled when the latter is true.)

One of the most eloquent ways we speak the language of love is through bearing the fruit of the Spirit. We must remember that fruit is for the benefit and nourishment of others. Spiritual fruit is what builds healthy relationships. No wonder Jesus cursed the barren fig tree (Matt. 21:19) and warned that fruitless branches would be cut off and cast into the furnace (John 15:6).

In most cases it doesn't take a lot to heal a relationship—a sincere apology, a little kindness and courtesy, some understanding of the other's point of view. Not much to ask and yet too often we stubbornly refuse to take the initiative; we won't admit our wrong, confess our sin. So, instead of a restoration and reconciliation, there is, at best, a standoff; and at worst, a divorce or alienation.

The devil does his best to build walls of isolation and separation between us, walls that stop or at least greatly hinder effective communication. Sometimes we don't know how to handle those walls. We can't get over them, around them, or tunnel under them. And it takes two (one on each side) to finally tear them down; so we figure we have to live with them. But there is a wonderful solution to the wall problem we may not have considered.

Recorded in Genesis 49 is the story of the dying patriarch Jacob calling his twelve sons before him to bestow his final blessings. It is interesting to see how he characterized each of those sons. In verse 22 he spoke to his favorite son, Joseph: "Joseph is a fruitful vine, a fruitful vine near a spring, whose branches climb over a wall." Despite all the obstacles that Joseph faced during his lifetime, especially the wall of alienation from his brothers, he was always a fruitful vine. He lived an upright, productive life. The way he handled walls was to let his fruitful branch climb over the wall. What a beautiful illustration of how to cope with barriers that hinder relevant communication and productive relationships. Rather than curse the wall or beat against it, he sent his fruitful influence and attitude over the wall to bless whoever was on the other side, so that finally together they might tear it down.

In confessing our faults, we send our fruitful branch over the walls of bitterness, jealousy, and hatred and thus begin the process of healing in relationships.

LANGUAGE LESSON

For use in individual study or family devotions

1. Recall two or three occasions when someone you know admitted he or she was wrong and apologized. How did it make you feel?

2. Try to remember several occasions when someone you know (don't use names and don't use this as an occasion to attack someone secretly) was clearly wrong but failed to admit it or apologize.

3. Imagine the difference that could be made in each situation had the person heeded (or not heeded) the guideline *Confess Your Faults*.

Practice Forgiveness

Be kind and compassionate to one another, forgiving each other, just as in Christ God forgave you.

Ephesians 4:32

Bear with each other and forgive whatever grievances you may have against one another. Forgive as the Lord forgave you.

Colossians 3:13

S E V E N
Practice Forgiveness

It was obvious from her physical appearance that the woman was deeply depressed. Her face was gaunt and drawn; there were large dark circles under her eyes. Her disheveled hair matched her wrinkled and soiled dress.

I had never seen the lady before that day when she came to my office. She had heard me on the radio and had called for a counseling appointment. As she came in the door, she didn't look at me or say a word. Without sitting down, she came to my desk, opened a battered briefcase and dumped out an assortment of yellowed, dog-eared legal documents.

"I want you to tell me what to do about these," she said.

I told her it would be impractical for me to sort through all the papers, so I needed her to sit down and explain the problem. Her story was a litany of bitterness, hatred, jealousy, and family feuding. The longer she talked the more emotionally involved she became until finally her sobbing made it impossible for her to continue.

She related how five years before, her family had cheated her out of a $4,500 inheritance. She had spent much time and money since then fighting her brothers and sisters in the courts — all to no avail. She was physically, mentally, and spiritually drained. When she regained her composure she made an incredible statement.

"You know what I do every morning before anything else? I take these documents out of the drawer and read them again. I don't ever want to forget what my family has done to me!"

No wonder she was severely depressed and on the verge of nervous collapse — or even death. Every day she was feeding her spirit a deadly dose of bitter memories and she was perpetuating the unforgiving hatred that was destroying her.

I admonished her to get rid of the legal documents, forgive her family, and put the matter behind her. However, even after further discussion and prayer together, she wanted to know if I could recommend a good lawyer. I never saw her again, but a few months later I found her name in the obituary column — a tragic casualty of an unforgiving spirit.

In recent years, numerous studies have established a direct connection between a bitter attitude and an array of physical problems. We cannot afford — physically, mentally, or spiritually — to ignore the clear scriptural command: "Bear with each other and forgive whatever grievances you may have against one another" (Col. 3:13).

It is impossible to communicate in a positive sense with others if we are unwilling to forgive. Forgiveness is one of the most powerful words in the language of love.

THE MUTUALITY OF FORGIVENESS

God doesn't make any bones about it: if we do not forgive, we will not be forgiven. When we have an unforgiving attitude, we feel somehow God doesn't really mean what he says or that he will give some special dispensation in our case. That is a dangerous assumption. His command is crystal clear: "If you do not forgive men their sins, your Father will not forgive your sins" (Matt. 6:15).

Forgiveness is an act of the will and it is unconditional. In human relationships it is not based upon the behavior of the other person (his request for forgiveness or his unforgiveness to us). It is not dictated by the kind of offense, and it is not limited in the number of times it is extended. From a human perspective these provisions blow our mind. We keep wanting to add conditions that seem reasonable to us. But God doesn't add conditions; he simply says, in all situations, at all times — forgive. That unconditional aspect of forgiveness is what makes it so powerful.

There are some things about forgiveness we need to keep in mind. (1) *Forgiveness does not imply ap-*

proval of the act committed. Because God forgives us of our sins does not mean he winks at those sins. Forgiveness is not predicated on the offense; it is an arbitrary act of mercy. (2) *It is hypocritical not to forgive.* Jesus makes this very plain in the parable of the unmerciful servant (Matt. 18:23-34). If God loved us enough to forgive us, we must love one another enough to forgive any grievance. (3) *If we don't forgive, we will suffer.* Like so many other aspects of our behavior, forgiveness is a two-edged sword. If we obey, we are blessed; if we disobey, we are cursed. When we fail to forgive, not only do we hurt the other person, but we open ourselves to great mental and spiritual anguish (Matt. 18:34-35).

In their book *Happiness Is a Choice,* Frank Minirth and Paul Meier list six groups of people who are often the object of anger and need to be forgiven:

> *First, there is often much repressed anger toward our parents. We need to remember that God can cause difficult situations in the past to work for our advantage, and that for the Christian all things work together for good. We need to remember that we too will make mistakes in raising our children. We need to forgive our parents for mistakes and sins they committed in the past when they were raising us, whether they deserve our forgiveness or not.*
>
> *Secondly, we need to forgive ourselves. Just*

as we get angry with other people, we become angry with ourselves for not doing better and making few mistakes. We are often critical with ourselves and are harder on ourselves than we are on other people. We need to forgive ourselves for past mistakes and sins. God is aware of our weaknesses. He knows we are but dust (Psalm 103:14). He says that when he removes our sins, they are as far from us as the east is from the west (v. 12). He wants us to do the same and no longer hold our past mistakes against ourselves.

Thirdly, we need to deal with our repressed anger toward God. We do not forgive God, for God has done nothing wrong; but we may have repressed anger or bitter feelings toward him. We may subconsciously reason in our mind somewhat as follows: After all, he is God, and he could have prevented or corrected the situation if he had chosen to. *Like Job we need to confess our anger toward God, talk with him about it, and ask him to help us resolve it.*

Fourthly, we need to deal with repressed anger toward our mate. We need to forgive him for mistakes he has made. When two individuals live together for many years, many anger-arousing situations occur, and anger can build up over a period of years and years. An individual needs to forgive in order to prevent depression.

Fifthly, we need to forgive those in authority over us. Anger often builds toward authority figures in our lives. We need to forgive them for whatever wrong we feel they may have done us. God has put them in authority over us. We need to respond to them and learn to talk with them about how we feel. Under no circumstances should we hold grudges against them.

The sixth category of those whom we need to forgive is simply classified as "others." There are often many other people in our lives whom we need to forgive. This group may include our peers when we were young. Various situations may have occurred then, and the repressed feelings and anger were never dealt with. The anger needs to be confessed and the person(s) forgiven.

Nothing is more strengthening to a relationship than to know what wrongs have been forgiven. The act of forgiveness tears down the wall that separates people. Even as the veil of the temple was rent when Christ died to bring forgiveness and redemption, giving man access to God in a brand-new way, forgiveness removes the barrier between people and provides a new avenue for communication.

Knowing we are forgiven, that there is now no hindrance to a positive relationship, gives us a joy that is inexpressible. With great exuberance David sang a joyful song as he contemplated the benefits of God—especially his forgiveness:

Praise the Lord, O my soul;
all my inmost being, praise his holy name.
Praise the Lord, O my soul,
and forget not all his benefits —
who forgives all your sins
and heals all your diseases,
who redeems your life from the pit
and crowns you with love and compassion,
who satisfies your desires with good things
so that your youth is renewed like the
* eagle's. . . .*
He does not treat us as our sins deserve
or repay us according to our iniquities.
For as high as the heavens are above the earth,
so great is his love for those who fear him;
as far as the east is from the west,
so far has he removed our transgressions
from us. (Psalm 103:1-5, 10-12)

When we know there is nothing between us in a relationship, it sweeps away the feelings of doubt, fear, and condemnation. It gives a freedom of communication and interaction not possible before.

I saw that truth demonstrated vividly a few years ago. A man who was afflicted with an unexplainable palsylike malady came to me for counseling. He had lost so much weight he looked like a walking skeleton. The doctors could not explain his condition, but they warned it would be fatal if it continued to progress.

The man's physical condition was critical, but his

spiritual state was even worse. He told me he had been a successful pastor for a number of years. Somehow he began to drift from God but made no effort to repent. Although he continued in the ministry, his spiritual state got worse and worse until finally the bottom dropped out. His church was taken from him and his ministry was lost. All that he had worked for was gone.

As he sank lower spiritually, the physical affliction came upon him. In his despair he cried out to God and repented with many tears; however, he could sense no forgiveness. For months he pleaded with God, seemingly to no avail. Now in his conversation with me, he expressed his desperation. "I know I'm going to die," he said, "and if I die, I'll go straight to hell."

I showed him in the Scriptures God's promise to forgive him. He knew all the Scriptures, but couldn't believe them for himself. As he talked, tears streamed down his face. I felt so inadequate to help. All of a sudden, the Spirit of God spoke to me, saying, "Tell my son I have already forgiven him. Tell him to stand on his feet, look me in the face, and declare, 'I am clean, I am pure, I am free!' "

I interrupted my friend and told him what the Lord had said. He was hesitant, but at my urging he stood up, looked toward the ceiling, and haltingly said, "OK, God. I'm going to try it." Then very slowly he stammered, "I am clean . . . I am pure . . . I am free." His face brightened a bit and he said it again, this time more confidently. The third time he said it, he began to cry and a big smile lighted up his face. The truth of his forgiveness had broken through to him. In that moment the thought struck me, *You can stand with your brother and make the same declaration.* I put my arm around his shoulder and we shouted together, "I am clean! I am pure! I am free!" For several minutes we had our own private camp-meeting service. Rejoicing was the order of the day.

As I recall that experience, I can still sense the joy and freedom we both felt. The realization of his forgiveness turned that man's life around. His physical symptoms eventually disappeared and he began taking steps to regain his ministry.

As God in his mercy sets us free and gives us the unspeakable joy of a right relationship with him, we have the responsibility and privilege to set free those in our lives who may be bound by the cords of our unforgiving attitude. "Be kind and compassionate to one another, forgiving each other, just as in Christ God forgave you" (Eph. 4:32).

Speak the language of love to someone today: "I forgive you!"

THE POSSIBILITY OF FORGETTING

The greatest proof of true forgiveness is in how the matter is handled "after the fact." God doesn't leave any doubt about what he does with our offenses once they are forgiven. He casts them behind his back to remember them against us no more (Isa. 38:17). He forgets them forever.

On the human level things are different. We boldly

state, "I'll forgive, but I won't forget." Even if we try to forget those forgiven offenses, the devil knows how to bring them up at the most appropriate (?) times.

A husband and wife get into a heated discussion. The wife, in trying to make her point with as much emphasis as possible, throws in a subject that obviously strikes a sensitive chord in her husband. "Why in the world would you bring that up?" he demands. "That happened before we got married. I thought you said you had forgiven me."

"I know," she says, "but I wanted to remind you *one more time.*"

We are good at remembering where the hatchet is buried. But we should know that every time we unearth it and use it again, the blade is blunter and it hurts more. Do we have to be reminded that every time we dig up the old garbage its odor is worse?

I heard about a businessman who went to see a psychiatrist about his wife. "Doc," he said, "you have got to help my wife. Every time we get into an argument, she gets *historical.*"

"No, no," the doctor corrected, "you mean she gets *hysterical.*"

"No, I mean she gets *historical.* She always brings up the past."

We may smile at that illustration, but the sad truth is, it is no laughing matter when we are reminded, especially at a time of high emotion, of our past mistakes and sins. While it is not reasonable to expect us to forget those things we say we have forgiven, there is one very practical way we can demonstrate our commitment. If we really have forgiven a matter, *we should never bring it up again*. That is quite a challenge, but certainly one possible for us to meet because we have total control over the words of our mouth.

The apostle Paul used his letter to the church at Philippi to deal with relationships. If anyone had a reason to remember past wrongs, it was Paul. But this epistle rings with joy—especially in Paul's testimony of his relationship to Christ and in his expression of love for the saints. In Philippians he gave a personal formula which can be of help in rejecting the temptation to bring up the past (3:12-14).

Notice these three steps: (1) *Practice humility.* Paul said that he was not perfect (v. 12). He did not claim to have reached all his personal goals. We will be more forgiving and less apt to hold grudges when we understand that we all are in a state of construction. God is not finished with us yet. (2) *Forget past hurts.* Paul had had many negative experiences, and he acknowledged he had enemies (some even in the church at Philippi), but he said he would forget what was behind (v. 13). Mulling over past hurts feeds an unforgiving attitude. (3) *Focus on the future.* Rather than always looking over his shoulder, Paul decided to focus on his goals (v. 14). It is difficult to harbor resentment and remember past wrongs when we are occupied with contemplating a bright future.

It is possible to *forgive and forget* if we follow the right rules. Joseph is a shining example of a man of God who not only forgave all the wrongs he experienced, but also demonstrated his determination to forget those things. It is recorded in Genesis that he named his firstborn son Manasseh, which means, "God has made me forget all my trouble" (41:51). Someone has admonished, "Write injuries in dust and benefits in marble."

THE BEAUTY OF FORBEARANCE

"Bear with each other" (see Eph. 4:2). *Forbearance.* Not as well known as some of the other terms we have discussed, but one of the most beautiful words in the language of love. It means "self-control, patience, restraint." In this context its simple and direct meaning is "putting up with each other."

A legal definition of forbearance is "extending the deadline for payment." That's great! What a wonderful application to human relationships. We have too many Ebenezer Scrooges around, who exact every relationship payment precisely when it is due. No flexibility, no allowance for weakness, pressure, or any other extenuating circumstance. We would all be in trouble if God operated that way.

If we have a happy marriage, if we do a decent job raising our kids, if we are a light to this world—we must put up with people. We must learn to accommodate and make allowances for one another. "Be completely humble and gentle; be patient, bearing with one another in love" (v. 2).

The emphasis of the secular humanistic movement on individual rights and self-actualization flies in the face of this plain scriptural imperative. We have a hard time putting up with people because they get in the way of what we want for ourselves. No true mother worried about her "rights" when a child was sick. No true friend ever was concerned about his own neck when a buddy was in danger.

How wonderful it would be if we would give our mate room to grow in new ways! How our children would love us if we would understand their differences and let them be themselves! How much more effective would our church be if we would open our arms to everyone and not expect them to fit our little molds!

As a final note, here is another line from the apostle Paul: "Do nothing out of selfish ambition or vain conceit, but in humility consider others better than yourselves. Each of you should look not only to your own interests, but also to the interests of others" (Phil. 2:3-4).

That's the language of love!

LANGUAGE LESSON

For use in individual study or family devotions

1. Think of one of the last times you realized you had wronged someone and tried to apologize.

How did the wronged person respond to your apology? What do you wish that person would have done? Are you satisfied with the way you responded? Why, or why not?

2. Try to recall one of the last times you were hurt by someone who had wronged you and didn't apologize. Are you satisfied with the way you responded? Were you angry? How did you express it?

3. What are some of the effects of unforgiveness on the offender? on the offended?

4. What are some of the causes of unforgiveness?

Love

G U I D E L I N E   8
Eliminate Nagging

When words are many, sin is not absent, but he who holds his tongue is wise.

Proverbs 10:19

A quarrelsome wife is like a constant dripping on a rainy day; restraining her is like restraining the wind or grasping oil with the hand.

Proverbs 27:15-16

As charcoal to embers and as wood to fire, so is a quarrelsome man for kindling strife.

Proverbs 26:21

E I G H T
Eliminate Nagging

I had just finished speaking to a large church group when a woman rushed up, cornered me between two pews, and launched into a nonstop barrage of words. Without the hint of a pause between sentences, she proceeded to tell me about her no-good husband, who recently had left her, and her two wayward daughters, one of whom was about to get a divorce.

Her emotions ran the gamut from intense anger to weeping frustration. She told me how lonely and depressed she was. She complained that her husband and daughters very seldom came to see her anymore. However, she assured me that when they did come, she let them know in no uncertain terms how displeased God was with them. She told them that unless they changed their ways, they were going straight to hell. "They can never say I didn't warn them. I don't want their blood on my hands." She was now running at full tilt, pointing her finger right at me. I thought I sensed a little of what her husband and daughters must have felt many times.

After about ten minutes, she finally paused and asked me a question. "I've done my best," she said. "What more can I do?"

Before she could answer her own question, I seized the initiative. "My sister," I said, "I believe I can help, but I don't want you to be offended." She assured me she wouldn't be. "You have simply got to stop talking so much and start demonstrating your love for your family in other ways." She seemed surprised, but she wanted to know what I meant.

I suggested that the next time her husband came to see her she fix his favorite meal and encourage him to talk about himself and his feelings. She should not be negative or critical in any of her words. I reminded her how much her daughters needed her love and personal support, especially as they were experiencing traumatic events in their own lives.

In general, I told her I didn't think she should preach to her family members anymore. She should pray for them, love them, be kind and considerate to them, but leave the convicting of their sinful ways to the prodding of the Holy Spirit. This didn't mean she had to condone or approve anything they were doing wrong. It did mean she had to stop pushing her own points and start paying attention to their needs.

In this chapter we come back to the basic premise of chapter 1: stop talking and start listening. If we are to speak the language of love, we must stop spouting our own line — especially in a nagging and contentious way. "Don't talk so much. You keep putting your foot in your mouth. Be sensible and turn off the flow!" (Prov. 10:19, TLB).

THE FUTILITY OF NAGGING

Nagging is a waste of time. Wise men don't need it and fools won't hear it. It is an exercise in futility. Yet all of us are guilty of practicing it — some much more than others.

Nagging doesn't work for a number of reasons. First of all, it is a selfish and egotistical behavior. It focuses attention on self — our opinions, our ideas, our attitudes. It imposes on others' time. We are taking their time (usually an exorbitant amount of it) to push our point. That isn't being fair or courteous.

When we are constantly speaking our point of view, we are missing hearing what others have to say. And if we are to relate to others as we should, we absolutely must hear what they have to say. "A fool finds no pleasure in understanding but delights in airing his own opinions" (Prov. 18:2).

One of the classic episodes in the life of Carol Burnett's character "Eunice" portrayed the reaction of the family to the visit of a long-absent, but now-famous, brother. At first they were very happy to see him; they wanted to hear all about his accomplishments. But as he began to tell them, they got more interested in talking and finally loudly arguing about their pet poodle. They never did hear his story. One of the reasons that episode was so funny was because it was unfortunately so true to life.

Another reason why nagging is futile is that it is downright boring. Usually we have heard it all before – many times. We can mimic (and sometimes do) the words and even the gestures. The Bible describes it as like the constant dripping of water (Prov. 19:13). "A constant dripping on a rainy day and a cranky woman are much alike! You can no more stop her complaints than you can stop the wind or hold onto anything with oil-slick hands" (Prov. 27:15-16, TLB).

Nagging is so annoying that our first reaction is to run away. In colorful language the Scriptures pick up on that feeling. (It might be noted that even though the following Scriptures refer to a contentious or nagging *woman,* gender has nothing to do with the problem, as we shall see later.) "It is better to live in the corner of an attic than with a crabby woman in a lovely home" (Prov. 21:9, TLB). "Better to live in the desert than with a quarrelsome, complaining woman" (21:19, TLB).

Not only is nagging selfish and boring, it is also counterproductive. It simply doesn't work. In fact, it usually backfires. Rather than producing the positive action intended, it often stirs anger or brings alienation. If we are not careful, we will be fooled into believing the longer we talk and the louder we talk, the more we are making our point. The problem is we are making a point, but not the one we intended.

The basic fallacy of nagging is that it features *talking,* and, as the Bible points out, talking is not the best way to speak the language of love. The ears, not the mouth, are the best instruments of communication. It has been well said, "The ears are not made to shut, but the mouth is."

THE PERIL OF CONTENTION

The practice of nagging lends itself to complaint and contention. The Bible says, "When words are many, sin is not absent" (Prov. 10:19). If we keep talking long enough, we will eventually say something we shouldn't – something negative, something sinful.

The derivation of the term *nag* is from a root word meaning "to nibble or gnaw." The word itself means "to annoy by continual scolding, faultfinding, complaining, urging." It is this character of complaint and contention that makes this practice so disposed to sinfulness. The damage done by contention is most noticeable in three particular areas:

A contentious spirit is offensive. Regardless of the intent, a quarrelsome, complaining attitude is received personally and negatively. For the Christian, any behavior that offends must be eliminated (Matt. 18:6-7). We should not engage in any action that might cause someone to sin or become disillusioned.

Unfortunately, all too often a contentious spirit is displayed when subjects of a spiritual nature are discussed. The worst kind of contention is that which is reinforced by a supposed scriptural sanction. The Pharisees of Jesus' day offended people by their harshness and insensitivity—and they justified that behavior by proudly declaring they were upholding and protecting the law of Moses.

The legalists of our day seem to believe that hardness is holiness. Their behavior actually turns mean when they are crossed about some of their religious beliefs. They defend their viewpoint of Scripture by imposing upon the feelings and time of others. Such behavior is particularly hurtful when it comes from family members or from those who are supposed to be Christian brothers and sisters.

While we have a right and a responsibility to express our viewpoints, we must always do so in a spirit of love and with a respect for the viewpoints of others. Any instruction must be given gently. Rather than an offending flow of contentious words, a life lived in demonstration of Christian principles most powerfully changes others for the better.

God will hold accountable those we cause to sin by our contentious attitude and demeanor. "Woe to the world because of the things that cause people to sin! Such things must come, but woe to that man through whom they come!" (Matt. 18:7). "It is harder to win back the friendship of an offended brother than to capture a fortified city. His anger shuts you out like iron bars" (Prov. 18:19, TLB).

A contentious spirit stirs up strife. When we continue to push our point of view, especially when we do it in a contentious, quarrelsome manner, we are going to make people mad. This is a mistake often made by a mate who is a Christian, trying to make a point with an unsaved partner. It matters not the content of your nagging approach — you may even be quoting Scripture verses — it will stir up anger in that unsaved mate. We will see later in this chapter that even witnessing can sometimes be more powerful *without* words.

A parent who constantly nags or pushes a child — for whatever reason — is treading on dangerous ground. We defeat our own purpose in training and discipline when we kindle the flame of anger in our children. "Now a word to you parents. Don't keep on scolding and nagging your children, making them angry and resentful. Rather, bring them up with the loving discipline the Lord himself approves, with suggestions and godly advice" (Eph. 6:4, TLB).

A contentious spirit harms our testimony. The people we interact with have a right to expect our behavior to match our testimony. There is perhaps nothing more disillusioning than interacting with someone who calls himself a Christian and finding that, at the personal level, there are displayed more "works of the flesh" than "fruit of the Spirit." No matter how we cut it, a Christian is supposed to be kind, considerate, humble, and gentle. When there is instead a contentious, quarrelsome, bad-tempered attitude, it comes as a shock, however "sophisticated" we may be about these things. And the greatest shock of all takes place when we experience these inconsistencies at the family level — with the people we know best and love most.

Here is an excerpt from a letter I received from

an offended husband. It brings this matter of a contentious spirit right down to ground level.

> *January 1 is the date I have set to leave my wife, the woman I married forty-one years ago. I made a terrible mistake in marrying this woman and it didn't take me long to find out I had. I tried to leave her before any children came along but my mother talked me into staying with her. This decision has cost me many years of unhappiness. My life has been one long hell.*
>
> *I did not know it at the time we married but my wife was a member of a family who quarreled and bellyached about everything and could see nothing good in anybody. I rejoiced when my wife informed me Christ had saved her, thinking surely to God life would be different living with a Christian, but I soon found out getting saved does not necessarily mean things will be better in a home.*
>
> *My wife has never respected me and when our son married she moved out of the bedroom telling me she no longer wanted to be a wife to me but only wanted to keep house for me. This she has failed to do also.*
>
> *Solomon says in Proverbs 12:4, "A virtuous woman is a crown to her husband, but she that maketh ashamed is as rottenness in his bones." It's hard to believe a Christian could cause any-*

> *body's bones to rot but that is what has hap-*
> *pened to me. That is what my wife has done to*
> *me.*
>
> *Now the reason I'll be leaving her the 1st of*
> *January is that is when I plan to retire from my*
> *job. She has a job and I'll give her my home*
> *all paid for. (That's all she wants from me any-*
> *way.) I'll try to start over somewhere else on*
> *my Social Security and pension. I would ask*
> *you to pray for us but it's too late; the die is set.*
> *She has destroyed me and now all I want is* out.

While we must receive instruction from examples such as this, we should keep in mind that this kind of experience is the exception rather than the rule. The majority of Christians are striving to do a better job speaking the language of love.

THE WONDER OF ATTENTION

As we have seen, we must eliminate nagging, with its complaining and contentious spirit, because it focuses attention on self rather than on the other person. We cannot possibly understand what is happening with others if we don't consciously focus our attention on them. If we do not know what is going on, we cannot help. There is no greater demonstration of love than to give attention. It is the highest form of compliment.

Jesus told the inquiring lawyer that the greatest of all the commandments was to "love the Lord your

God with all your heart and with all your soul and with all your mind . . . and . . . love your neighbor as yourself" (Matt. 22:37-39). As a follow-up question, the lawyer asked, "Who is my neighbor?" In answering, Jesus told the story of the Good Samaritan. Read it again.

> *In reply Jesus said: "A man was going down from Jerusalem to Jericho, when he fell into the hands of robbers. They stripped him of his clothes, beat him and went away, leaving him half dead. A priest happened to be going down the same road, and when he saw the man, he passed by on the other side. So too, a Levite, when he came to the place and saw him, passed by on the other side. But a Samaritan, as he traveled, came where the man was; and when he saw him, he took pity on him. He went to him and bandaged his wounds, pouring on oil and wine. Then he put the man on his own donkey, took him to an inn and took care of him.*
>
> *"The next day he took out two silver coins and gave them to the innkeeper. 'Look after him,' he said, 'and when I return, I will reimburse you for any extra expense you may have.'*
>
> *"Which of these three do you think was a neighbor to the man who fell into the hands of robbers?"*
>
> *The expert in the law replied, "The one who had mercy on him." (Luke 10:30-37)*

Embodied in this parable are four basic laws of positive human relationships—four primary ways to speak the language of love:

Availability. "He . . . came where the man was." Instead of passing by on the other side as the priest and Levite had done, the Good Samaritan stopped and came where he was. We can minister to people only when we come where they are, in body and in spirit.

Attention. "He saw him." The implication here is that he did more than *look* at him. The priest and Levite did that. He paid attention and noticed what was happening with this wounded traveler. Sometimes we have eyes to see, but we don't see; we don't pay close attention to what is going on with other people. When we know those we interact with "after the Spirit," we will be in a much better position to help them.

Attitude. "He took pity on him." When he saw the condition of the man, it touched his heart. He was moved with compassion. After we sense the needs people have, we must be moved by a loving attitude toward them. Bob Pierce, founder of World Vision, put it like this: "Let my heart be broken with the things that break the heart of God."

Action. "He . . . bandaged up his wounds." He didn't just feel for the man or tell him he loved him and would be praying for him, he did something to demonstrate his love. That is always the bottom-line test of our love for others: what are we willing to do for them?

Availability, attention, attitude, action. Check the relationships you have with those closest to you against these four principles.

A powerfully significant Scripture beautifully summarizes the idea of using attitude and attention, *without words,* to win an unsaved mate: "Wives, in the same way be submissive to your husbands so that, if any of them do not believe the word, they may be won over without talk by the behavior of their wives, when they see the purity and reverence of your lives" (1 Pet. 3:1-2).

Daniel Schantz, writing in *Guideposts* (March 1987), tells of watching a deaf-mute making a purchase in a jewelry store. That experience led him to the discovery of some principles that give the ability to "speak volumes without words."

> Look at people. *Don't just look toward people, look at them. Eye contact is vital.*
> Touch someone. *A touch on the arm or shoulder says, "I'm not afraid to get close to you." Jesus touched even lepers.*
> Linger a little. *Make your contacts unhurried. Even a few extra seconds of undivided attention can make a big difference.*
> Imagine. *Imagine what the other person's life is like. Imagine what his concerns are.*
> Let others love you. *Communication is not a one-way street. Others need a chance to help us and we shouldn't be ashamed to mention our needs.*

Speaking volumes without words—without nagging, complaints, or contentions. That is the way to speak the language of love.

LANGUAGE LESSON

For use in individual study or family devotions

1. Think of one of the last experiences you had with trying to urge someone to do something. How successful were you? What did you do wrong? What did you do right? How could you have done better?

2. Try to recall one of the last times you felt some-one was nagging you. Were you hurt by this person who failed to exercise the guideline explained in this chapter? What do you wish that person would have done? Are you satisfied with the way you responded? Why, or why not?

3. What are some of the things a person can do to avoid developing a contentious spirit? Think of someone who recently demonstrated this important principle about showing the language of love. What can you learn from that person?

Love

GUIDELINE 9
Be Constructive, Not Critical

Therefore let us stop passing judgment on one another. Instead, make up your mind not to put any stumbling block or obstacle in your brother's way.

Romans 14:13

Brother, if someone is caught in a sin, you who are spiritual should restore him gently. But watch yourself, or you also may be tempted.

Galatians 6:1

N I N E
Be Constructive, Not Critical

Several years ago, while visiting my parents at their home in California, I had a chance encounter that left an indelible impression upon me. A man had come to my parents' home to repair their automatic washer. As he was working on the machine, I struck up a conversation with him.

In the course of the conversation, I happened to mention that I was a minister. Lying on his back, with his head out of sight at the back of the washer, the man remarked rather disgustedly, "I used to be a minister myself." He went on to say that he had been the pastor of a certain church in that city—a church I knew to be one of the largest, most prominent evangelical congregations in the area.

My curiosity was aroused. I asked him the inevitable question: "If you were called to be a pastor, how is it that you are now working as an appliance repairman?"

The man rolled out from behind the washer, sat up, and laid his tools aside. He looked me in the eye and spoke very deliberately. "I'll tell you why I got out of the ministry. I got sick and tired of some of the people in the church with their bad attitudes and vicious criticisms." He told how some church leaders had been particularly critical of his wife and family. "It was bad enough when they criticized me," he said, "but when they started on my wife and kids, I decided that was too much." The pain of his decision was obvious as he recounted the story.

After an extended conversation, the man finally finished his work and was gone. I was left to ponder the meaning of what I had heard. While I did not necessarily agree with the way this former pastor had handled his problems, I did identify with the pain and anguish he and his family had suffered. As he talked about his experiences, I was reminded again of the destructiveness of criticism—of the sting caused by the acid tongue.

While nagging is characterized as "gnawing or nibbling," criticism is described as "biting and devouring." Listen to the apostle Paul writing to the Galatians: "The entire law is summed up in a single command: 'Love your neighbor as yourself.' If you keep on biting and devouring each other, watch out or you will be destroyed by each other" (5:14-15). *The Living Bible* translates verse 15: "But if instead of showing love among yourselves you are always critical and catty, watch out! Beware of ruining each other."

I wonder if some of those church leaders who spoke so critically were not guilty of "ruining" that former pastor and his family. When the Bible says "watch out" or "beware," we had best take heed. The language of love can never be communicated with a critical tongue or judgmental spirit.

THE DESTRUCTIVENESS OF CRITICISM

It is much easier to be critical than to be constructive. There is much in our world — in our family, in our church, on our job — of which to be critical. However, when we really understand the destructive nature of criticism, we should be motivated to refrain from making critical comments.

To put the matter in simple terms: when we are critical and judgmental, we are doing the devil's work. It is the devil who is the accuser (Rev. 12:10). He is the one who condemns, criticizes, judges, points the finger, and shifts the blame. One of the reasons why we are so sensitive to criticism from others is that we are constantly bombarded with messages of guilt, accusation, and condemnation from the evil one. Satan is characterized as a great enemy, prowling around "like a hungry, roaring lion, looking for some victim to tear apart" (1 Pet. 5:8, TLB).

Critical words do just that: they tear the victim apart, especially when the criticism comes from someone close, someone looked up to, someone loved. It is like a sword that cuts deeply into the spirit, like a dagger that plunges to the depth of self-esteem, like a dart that wounds a tender heart. As Christians, we should never be guilty of wielding such weapons.

Children are particularly vulnerable to criticism. They are deeply involved in that delicate process of determining self-worth. They are looking and listening for clues that tell them who and what they are. When parents or other authority figures put them down, the resulting negative impressions can last a lifetime. Think of how some of these common parental put-downs affect a child's view of himself: "Won't you ever learn?" "What a stupid thing to do!" "How many times do I have to tell you?" "What ever will become of you?" "Now, look what you did"; "I don't know what I'm going to do with you"; "You make me sick."

Obviously, it is not possible to be involved with children or with others without periodically confronting negative situations. All we communicate to others cannot be positive and complimentary. However, it is when we attack the *person* rather than the *problem* that great damage is done. It is very important when it is necessary to correct or discipline that we concentrate on the behavior and not the behaver. The Scripture teaches us to despise the sin, yet love the sinner. It is when this line between the performance and the person is disregarded that constructive correction can become destructive criticism.

This distinction is important in any relationship but is vital in dealing with children. It is very difficult for children to distinguish between sources of criticism as adults generally do. As adults, with many of the negative comments directed at us, we are able to consider the source and thus minimize any psychological or spiritual damage. Not so with children. They tend to receive all verbal and non-verbal responses at face value.

Dorothy Law Noite, in her poem, "Children Learn What They Live," speaks of the life-forming power of a child's environment:

> *If a child lives with criticism,*
> *he learns to condemn.*
> *If a child lives with hostility,*
> *he learns to fight.*
> *If a child lives with fear,*
> *he learns to be apprehensive.*
> *If a child lives with pity,*
> *he learns to feel sorry for himself.*
> *If a child lives with ridicule,*
> *he learns to be shy.*
> *If a child lives with jealousy,*
> *he learns what envy is.*
> *If a child lives with shame,*
> *he learns to feel guilty.*
> *If a child lives with encouragement,*
> *he learns to be confident.*
> *If a child lives with tolerance,*
> *he learns to be patient.*
> *If a child lives with praise,*
> *he learns to be appreciative.*
> *If a child lives with acceptance,*
> *he learns to love.*

If a child lives with approval,
  he learns to like himself.
If a child lives with recognition,
  he learns that it is good to have a goal.
If a child lives with sharing,
  he learns about generosity.
If a child lives with honesty and fairness,
  he learns what truth and justice are.
If a child lives with security,
  he learns to have faith in himself and in those
    about him.
If a child lives with friendliness,
  he learns that the world is a nice place in
    which to live.
If you live with serenity,
  your child will live with peace of mind.

One of the chapters in Dale Carnegie's book, *How to Win Friends and Influence People,* is entitled, "If You Want to Gather Honey, Don't Kick Over the Bee-hive." What he meant was: "If you want to win friends, don't be critical." Like so many other violations of God's Word, not only is destructive criticism a sin, it also doesn't work. It is counter-productive.

Criticism stirs resentment that often lasts a life-time. The course of history has been changed be-cause of a lingering resentment over criticism, as with the celebrated public dispute between Theo-dore Roosevelt and William Howard Taft. On a level closer to home, think of the divorces caused, the children alienated, the friends separated because someone was careless with criticism.

The Bible lets us know in no uncertain terms that if we are to speak the language of love, we must refrain from criticism. "You have no right to criticize your brother or look down on him. Remember, each of us will stand personally before the judgment seat of God. For it is written, 'As I live,' says the Lord, 'every knee shall bow to me and every tongue confess to God.' Yes, each of us will give an account of himself to God. So don't criticize each other any more. Try instead to live in such a way that you will never make your brother stumble by letting him see you doing something he thinks is wrong" (Rom. 14:10-13, TLB).

THE NURTURE OF APPRECIATION

Mark Twain said, "I can live for two months on a sincere compliment."

Ted Engstrom, in his book, *The Fine Art of Friendship*, told of his habit of sending memos to his employees, especially to compliment them about their work. He recounts how one of his secretaries, upon her retirement after more than ten years of service, showed him a beautifully bound book that she had been putting together during the years she worked for him. When Ted opened the book, he found she had saved *every* memo he had sent her. She wanted to remember always every complimentary word.

Praise costs so little, yet we often use it so sparingly. When we know the good it does, why is it we are so stingy with praise? Why do we find it easier to criticize than to show appreciation? The answer lies within us. We project our faults on others. "You, therefore, have no excuse, you who pass judgment on someone else, for at whatever point you judge the other, you are condemning yourself, because you who pass judgment do the same things" (Rom. 2:1). It is said that those who are the most critical feel the most self-hate. It follows then that those who practice giving praise and appreciation feel good about themselves.

As criticism and accusation are the work of the devil, so are praise and appreciation the work of God. God's Word to his people is always constructive. Even in correction, his love is the predominant factor. As followers of God, we must seek to emulate his attitude in our relationships with others, beginning with those of our own household.

The Lord constantly reminds us he loves us — even when we displease or disobey him. In our failure and sin we receive no condemning or accusatory word from him. Our expression of love for those who fail us or sin against us powerfully demonstrates our love for God. A word of encouragement, forgiveness, or appreciation to someone who expects to be criticized or condemned can transform a relationship. A mate who has failed, a child who has disobeyed, a friend who has let us down — these expect a scathing rebuke. But if instead they receive a message that says, "What you did has hurt me, but I still love you," they are much more likely to turn their behavior around than if they had received strong criticism.

To be appreciative and understanding does not mean that we overlook or condone wrong behavior in others. It simply means we concentrate on the best in others rather than magnifying their faults. This is the way the Lord dealt with the failure of Peter. Though Peter denied him three times, there came no word of criticism or condemnation from Jesus. Rather, the Lord let Peter know he still loved him by sending a special message concerning his resurrection (Mark 16:7). The Lord was saying "Peter, I know you denied me, but that does not cancel out all you have done in the past; neither will it keep me from blessing you in the future. I forgive you." Peter responded by repenting of his wrongs, returning to the Lord's fellowship, and eventually going on to lead the church.

How much better is God's plan of restoration than the devil's program of retribution. "Dear brothers, if a Christian is overcome by some sin, you who are godly should gently and humbly help him back onto the right path, remembering that next time it might be one of you who is in the wrong" (Gal. 6:1, TLB).

Honest words of appreciation and a lack of criticism are not only edifying to the person spoken about but also to those who observe and hear. Recently I was involved in the funeral of a pastor who was known for his skill in telling stories. Kelland Jeffords could keep an audience, from one to hundreds, spellbound as he recounted in intimate detail, often with a humorous touch, the behavior of people he knew. He loved people, and he had a special insight into how they behaved. The most significant thing to me about Kelland's skill in storytelling was his ability to illustrate colorfully the uniqueness of human nature without ever being critical or poking fun. When he finished telling a story about a person, you felt good about that person and better about yourself. The outpouring of love and appreciation at his funeral (which was termed a "coronation") was strong testimony to the edifying way he talked about others.

Nothing builds self-esteem in others like honest praise and appreciation. If we want our family members to feel good about themselves we need to be hearty in our approbation and lavish in our praise. There is good reason why we love to have those dogs around who are always wagging their tails. Their behavior says, "I like you. You are my best friend." How much more meaningful is it to have a fellow human being say by his actions and by his words, "I love you and appreciate you. You are a worthwhile person." It is tragic that so many people *never* receive such messages, even from those closest to them. To compound the tragedy, usually those persons receive instead a constant barrage of criticism and accusation. Is it any wonder we have so many people in our society bound by feelings of inferiority, guilt, and insecurity?

In our humanistic world we are told the only way to rid ourselves of our negative feelings and troubles is to tap our inner resources — to pull ourselves up by our own bootstraps — to become "self-actualized." We are admonished to look out for "number one." The implication is that we should not expect nor do we need any "outside" help. There are two basic things we need to understand about that philosophy: it is wrong and it does not work.

The truth is, in our willingness to give of ourselves to others we find our own fulfillment. "Give, and it will be given to you. A good measure, pressed down, shaken together and running over, will be poured into your lap. For with the measure you use, it will be measured to you" (Luke 6:38).

St. Francis of Assisi beautifully illustrated this point in his poem "Eternal Life":

> *Lord, make me an instrument of your peace,*
> *Where there is hatred, let me sow love —*
> *Where there is injury, pardon —*
> *Where there is doubt, faith —*
> *Where there is despair, hope —*
> *Where there is darkness, light —*
> *Where there is sadness, joy.*
> *O Divine Master, grant that I may not so much seek*
> *To be consoled — as to console,*
> *To be understood — as to understand,*
> *To be loved — as to love,*
> *For*
> *It is in giving that we receive,*
> *It is in pardoning that we are pardoned,*

It is in dying that we are born to eternal life.

Appreciation and praise pay great dividends — to the receiver as well as to the giver. On the other hand accusation and criticism produce negative results. Listen again to the Word of God: "Never criticize or condemn — or it will all come back on you" (Luke 6:37, TLB).

If we are to speak the language of love, we would do well to determine as did Benjamin Franklin, "I will speak ill of no man and speak all the good I know of everybody."

THE PRINCIPLE OF CHANGE

One of the main reasons we criticize others is to produce change in them. We think if we tell our son how stupid he is for what he did, he will think twice before doing the same thing again. We have the idea if we berate our wife loudly enough and long enough, she will stop her annoying behavior. When our approach doesn't work, instead of searching for a better way, we tend to attack the problem with an amplified version of the same method.

We must come to understand that force does not produce desired change. God does not operate that way with us; we cannot operate that way with others. The only way change will come in others is if they are motivated to make it happen. We cannot produce the change, but we certainly can help with the motivation.

The most powerful instrument for change is love. That is the instrument God used to bring about the greatest change a man could ever experience—personal salvation. So great is this change that it is referred to as being "born again." In his wisdom God ordained that this experience could not be forced. We are not saved because God has railed against us in our sin; we are saved because in love he sent his only Son to die for us. It is his love, not his condemnation, that draws us to him.

The same principle applies in our effort to change others for the better. The only way this will happen is through our love as it is translated into loving words and deeds. To illustrate the practicality of this point in marital relationships, Paul admonished husbands to love their wives as Christ loved the church and *gave* himself for it (Eph. 5:25). He went on to say that the result of this giving by Christ was "perfection" or positive change in the church. In the same way and for the same reason, he says, husbands "ought to love their wives as their own bodies" (5:28).

Positive change is brought about by positive relationships. Just as when we draw closer to God, we become more like him; so when we draw closer to one another through mutual love, submission, and understanding, we will bring out the best in one another.

Positive relationships are nurtured through appreciation and praise; they are destroyed by accusation and criticism. The greatest stumbling block to positive relationships and positive change is a critical spirit and a judgmental attitude. "Therefore let us stop passing judgment on one another. Instead, make up your mind not to put any stumbling block or obstacle in your brother's way" (Rom. 14:13).

LANGUAGE LESSON

For use in individual study or family devotions

1. Try to recall at least two or three recent occasions when you realized *you* were becoming critical of someone.

2. Ask yourself, and perhaps share with someone else, why on those occasions you said or did things that reflected a critical spirit.

3. Try to think of ways you could have responded to demonstrate the language of love during those occasions.

4. Try to imagine how the other person would have responded to you if you had shown a more constructive approach.

Love

Leave Vengeance to God

Do not repay anyone evil for evil. Be careful to do what is right in the eyes of everybody.

Romans 12:17

Do not repay evil with evil or insult with insult, but with blessing, because to this you were called so that you may inherit a blessing.

1 Peter 3:9

T E N
Leave Vengeance to God

It is human to retaliate. Part of our defense system programs us to strike back when we are hit. But the Bible teaches against such behavior. God's law says we are not to return evil for evil or insult for insult. What do we do then when we are wronged? We turn the other cheek; we go the second mile; we return blessing for insult. Sound idealistic? impractical? crazy? Not only does God say such a response is possible; it is required.

Jesus dealt with this principle in a startling way early in his ministry. What he said is recorded in the book of Matthew:

> *You have heard that it was said, "Eye for eye, and tooth for tooth." But I tell you, Do not resist an evil person. If someone strikes you on the right cheek, turn to him the other also. And*

if someone wants to sue you and take your tunic, let him have your cloak as well. If someone forces you to go one mile, go with him two miles. Give to the one who asks you, and do not turn away from the one who wants to borrow from you. (5:38-42)

The practicality of Jesus' teaching was put to the test in his own life on several occasions. It has been proven in the crucible of human relationships through the centuries. It still works today.

On the family level the restraint of retaliation avoids nonproductive confrontations and prevents damaging arguments. It models temperance, patience, tolerance, and other positive forms of self-discipline. It demonstrates the power of Christ at work in a human heart. On the other hand, when this teaching is violated, it opens the door to an array of destructive forces.

THE PRINCIPLE OF VENGEANCE

The negative connotation of the term *vengeance* is seen in the words with which it is defined: "punishment, retribution, revenge, retaliation, with great force, to an extreme or excessive degree." The definition itself ought to explain why a Christian should not engage in this behavior. Vengeance is God's business, and we need to stay out of it. "Do not take revenge, my friends, but leave room for God's wrath, for it is written: 'It is mine to avenge; I will repay,' says the Lord" (Rom. 12:19). We don't have to worry;

justice will be done; God will repay. But God will deal with the matter equitably through his wisdom and mercy.

When we follow God's direction in withholding vengeance, we turn the person who has wronged us over to God. In this connection Paul quoted a passage from the book of Proverbs: "If your enemy is hungry, feed him; if he is thirsty, give him something to drink. In doing this, you will heap burning coals on his head" (Rom. 12:20; see also Prov. 25:21-22). Matthew Henry commented about the concept of "burning coals": "It will be a likely means to win upon them [our enemies] and bring them over to be reconciled to us; we shall mollify them as the refiner melts the metal in the crucible, not only by putting it over the fire, but by heaping coals of fire upon it."

I heard the story of a new convert who came across this passage in the Bible and went to his pastor for an interpretation. The pastor explained that the Lord was instructing us to do something good for someone we could not get along with and in so doing would heap coals of fire upon his head. The new convert was fascinated by this concept and immediately thought of it in connection with his next-door neighbor, who had been an enemy of long standing. He reckoned the most gracious thing he could do for his enemy was to weed his garden, which was quite overgrown. This he did before daylight the next morning.

When his enemy awoke, he was amazed to find his garden completely free of weeds. To his even greater amazement, he discovered it was his neighbor who had done the good deed. His curiosity aroused, he confronted the man and asked him the meaning of his behavior in view of their previous relationship.

"I have become a Christian," said the new convert, "and I learned in the Bible that if I would do a good deed for an enemy, it would heap coals of fire upon his head. Now I've done the deed for you and I hope it burns your brains out!" A *human* response to a *divine* principle.

When we are offended in our relationships, our feelings generally move through four stages: (1) hurt, (2) anger, (3) revenge, (4) destructive action/psychosomatic symptoms/depression. Each succeeding step tends to hide the preceding one. After the initial hurt, if the matter is not confronted and resolved, we become angry. If the anger is allowed to remain, it will eventually develop into an urge to seek revenge. Gary Collins describes how a vengeful attitude can manifest itself:

> *Revenge sometimes leads to destructive violent actions, but this can get us into trouble, and violence is not acceptable, especially for a Christian. As a result, some people try to hide their feelings. This takes energy, which wears down the body so that the emotions eventually come to the surface in the form of psychosomatic symptoms. Others, consciously or unconsciously, condemn themselves for their*

> *attitudes and become depressed as a result.*
> *This depression may be a form of emotional*
> *self-punishment, which sometimes even leads*
> *to suicide. It is easy to understand why such*
> *people feel that they are no good, guilty and*
> *unhappy.* (Christian Counseling)

When we allow a spirit of vengeance to grip us, we can easily be pushed into becoming verbally, and even physically, abusive. The Bible gives this admonition: "Do not say [of your neighbor], 'I'll do to him as he has done to me; I'll pay that man back for what he did' " (Prov. 24:29).

One of the best ways to neutralize the cycle, as the one mentioned above, which moves from hurt to destructive action, is to force ourselves back to the source of the hurt and deal with the problem at that level. If we would suffer the hurt as we are told to do, we would stop the matter from moving beyond that point. Every hurt does not have to move to anger, to revenge, to destructive action. We would seldom have to deal with violent behavior if we would exercise spiritual discipline at the beginning point of the offense.

In human relationships, we cannot fight fire with fire. If we attempt to do this, the spark of anger will flare into a mighty conflagration. When a conflict arises between husband and wife, it can develop into a game of "Can You Top This?" Each negative statement or catty remark is matched by one that tends to aggravate further the feeling of hostility. As with the crumbling dam described earlier, it is foolhardy to allow such an escalation to continue. Someone has to stop the cycle and allow the other to have the last word. Be warned that the longer such an exchange continues, the more difficult it is to stop. That is why it should never be allowed to start.

With children, the matter becomes more complicated. When a child returns a verbal dart, it is taken as rebellion or disrespect. Yet a parent often is responsible for eliciting that remark by his own behavior. According to the Scriptures, parents are not to exasperate their children. "And now a word to you parents. Don't keep on scolding and nagging your children, making them angry and resentful" (Eph. 6:4, TLB).

I once had a father bring his son to me for counseling. In his son's presence he proceeded to tell me how rebellious, lazy, disrespectful, and ungrateful his son was. When the son tried to make a point of his own, the father told him to shut up, and he lifted his hand to indicate he meant to physically enforce his will, if necessary. I interrupted his tirade and asked the son to leave the office. I told the father that from what I had observed in those few minutes, it was my opinion he was primarily responsible for his son's behavior. He was aggravating and exasperating his son. The father became extremely angry and threatened to walk out. Fortunately, he stayed and we were able to agree on a positive course of action, primarily involving a change in the father's behavior. In the weeks that followed I had the thrill of watching a son's attitude transformed because a father cared enough to face up to his own responsibilities.

When we seek revenge, hold grudges, or determine to "get even," we are committing sin and will inevitably reap the consequences. We are harming ourselves physically, mentally, and spiritually and are irreparably damaging our relationships with others.

God shows us a better way. "Don't repay evil for evil. Don't snap back at those who say unkind things about you. Instead, pray for God's help for them, for we are to be kind to others, and God will bless us for it" (1 Pet. 3:9, TLB).

THE GIVING OF BLESSINGS

Instead of returning insult for insult, we are told to give a blessing. That sounds pious and unrealistic until we remember that is what we are called to do as Christians. We are to build up rather than tear down. We are to repair and restore (Isa. 58:12). This command applies especially to conflict situations. "Bless those who persecute you; bless and do not curse" (Rom. 12:14).

Jesus practiced this principle when he was brought before his accusers. "When they hurled their insults at him, he did not retaliate; when he suffered, he made no threats. Instead, he entrusted himself to him who judges justly" (1 Pet. 2:23).

Blessing rather than retaliating immediately cools the hottest personal conflict. It brings a peace to the giver that can spread quickly to the others involved.

In marital and family relationships the effort can be almost miraculous.

A few years ago, I counseled a couple that was on the verge of divorce. They said they loved each other, yet they argued constantly. Even as they described their problem to me, they traded accusations until I thought they were going to attack one another physically right in my office.

The wife described how her husband arrived home from work every day precisely at 5:30 P.M., came in the back door (to avoid speaking to her), took a shower, read the paper, ate his supper (without comment), watched television, and finally, half asleep, fell into bed. Every day it was the same routine and weekends were worse.

The husband told his side of the story. Yes, it was true he came in the back door each day after work. That was because he didn't want to see his wife. Her hair was always in curlers, and she usually wore an old chenille bathrobe he hated. Neither did he want to talk to her because she always had a complaint. His life was one big bore.

I asked them if they ever did anything for one another. Did they give gifts? Go out together? Not in years, they said. They had fallen into a consistent pattern of putting each other down and doing nothing to build each other up. I suggested a radical plan of intervention. Neither of them thought it would work, but they reluctantly agreed to cooperate.

The next day, the husband was to stop by a florist

shop on the way home from work and pick up a bouquet for his wife. When he arrived home, he was to go in the *front* door, give his wife the flowers, and tell her he loved her.

The wife, first of all, was to get rid of her chenille bathrobe. The next day she was to get up early, clean the house, fix her husband's favorite meal, and then dress as if she were going out on a date. When she saw her husband arrive, she was to greet him at the front door and tell him she loved him.

They came back to see me the following week. They were beaming. The husband told how he had thought all that day about what was going to happen when he walked in with those flowers. His main worry was that maybe his wife would forget her part or wouldn't be willing to go through with the plan. She recounted how excited she was as she cleaned the house and fixed the meal. She also was proud of the way she looked. Her only worry was whether or not her husband would keep his end of the bargain. She told how she thought her heart was going to beat out of her chest as the clock rolled around to 5:30 P.M. Then she saw the car pull up in the driveway.

"When I saw him get out of that car with a bouquet of flowers in his hand, it was more than I could take," she said. Her husband interrupted. "I didn't even get to the front porch. She came flying out that door, threw her arms around my neck, and hugged me like I have never been hugged." A conscious act of giving literally transformed their relationship forever. They learned the miracle of blessing rather than cursing each other.

It is much easier, of course, when both partners are willing to give. However, with this principle of returning good for evil, the good behavior usually has to be initiated unilaterally. A beautiful scriptural example of this is seen in the life of Joseph. He had the reason and the power to take vengeance on his brothers for their evil deeds to him. But rather than use his position for revenge, he used it for restoration and reconciliation. The joy he experienced in having his family back together could never have happened had he not been willing to return good for evil.

Another eloquent way to speak the language of love is to give a blessing in return for an insult.

THE PROMISE OF REWARD

"Do not repay evil with evil or insult with insult, but with blessing, because to this you were called so that you may inherit a blessing" (1 Pet. 3:9). The proposition here is that if we bless we will be blessed. That is a major operational principle in God's law: "You will reap what you sow." Though this concept is more frequently used as a warning against sowing bad seed, it is also a wonderful promise to those who sow good seed.

Much of the confusion and conflict that dominates marriages and disrupts families is brought about because there is an obsession with getting even and little practice of "turning the other cheek." Anyone who has engaged in the game of getting even knows there are no winners. What the Lord is trying to tell us in this principle of "good for evil" is that to win we must lose — one of those theological concepts that is beyond human understanding. This idea is closely akin to some other teachings of Jesus: "The first shall be last and the last shall be first" and "In order to live, we must die."

It is not necessary for us to understand how these principles operate; our only obligation is to practice them and then sit back and watch them work. Not only do they work to God's glory, but also to our benefit.

The Lord says if we will return good for evil, we will inherit a blessing and we will live peaceably. Translated into practical, nitty-gritty terms, that means we will be happier in our marriage; there will be considerably less stress in our home; and there will be fewer arguments and greater harmony among our family members and friends. Our life overall will be much easier to live. That is quite a return on the small investment necessary to cut across the pattern of normal human behavior — to turn the other cheek, to go the second mile, to return good for evil.

Think of the powerful testimony such behavior gives. Without saying a word we speak eloquently to our mate, our children, and others what it means to be a Christian. What a lesson to our sons and daughters! But concerning rewards, think of the sense of satisfaction and the feeling of peace we receive when we practice this principle. Rather than the tenseness of retaliation, the bitterness of rebuke, and the depression that comes when angry confrontations finally end, we experience a fullness of joy that is unspeakable and full of glory.

Understand that such a reward does not come without a battle with the flesh. Our carnal nature rebels against anything that appears to give another "self" an advantage over us. The secret, of course, lies in the fact that we are not being used; we are not being taken advantage of; we are *giving* ourselves consciously for a higher purpose. We have the same control that Jesus had when he spoke of the sacrifice he was to make on the cross: "No one takes it [my life] from me, but I lay it down of my own accord" (John 10:18).

In allowing ourselves to be "used" in this way, we more fully understand ourselves and the true meaning of life. We become real. Without this willingness to forgo vengeance by returning good for evil, the very essence of life eludes us.

Margery Williams, in her fascinating children's story, *The Velveteen Rabbit,* described a scene in which a new toy in the nursery, a stuffed rabbit, receives a word of instruction about the meaning of life from the well-worn, but much-loved, stuffed horse:

> *"It doesn't happen all at once," said the Skin Horse. "You become. It takes a long time. That's why it doesn't often happen to people who break*

> *easily, or have sharp edges, or who have to be carefully kept. Generally, by the time you are Real, most of your hair has been loved off, and your eyes drop out and you get loose in the joints and very shabby. But these things don't matter at all, because once you are Real you can't be ugly, except to people who don't understand."*

If we are to speak the language of love as we should, we can't "break easily, or have sharp edges, or . . . be carefully kept." We must give ourselves to others, returning good for evil, for to this we are called so that we, in turn, may inherit a blessing (1 Pet. 3:9).

LANGUAGE LESSON

For use in individual study or family devotions

1. Think of one of the last times you were tempted to retaliate against someone who had wronged you. Are you satisfied with the way you responded? Why, or why not?

2. Try to recall one of the last times someone dealt with you on "an eye for an eye and a tooth for a tooth" basis. Are you satisfied with the way you responded to the retaliation? Were you angry? How did you express it?

3. What are some of the effects of unforgiveness on the offender? on the offended?

4. What are some of the things we can do to help us to practice the guideline *Leave Vengeance to God?*

G U I D E L I N E S

Stop Talking and Start Listening

Think Before You Speak

Speak the Truth in Love

Disagree, but Don't Argue

Control Your Response

Confess Your Faults

Practice Forgiveness

Eliminate Nagging

Be Constructive, Not Critical

Leave Vengeance to God

Other Living Books Best-sellers

400 CREATIVE WAYS TO SAY I LOVE YOU by Alice Chapin. Perhaps the flame of love has almost died in your marriage, or you have a good marriage that just needs a little spark. Here is a book of creative, practical ideas for the woman who wants to show the man in her life that she cares. 07-0919-5

ANSWERS by Josh McDowell and Don Stewart. In a question-and-answer format, the authors tackle sixty-five of the most-asked questions about the Bible, God, Jesus Christ, miracles, other religions, and Creation. 07-0021-X

THE BELOVED STRANGER by Grace Livingston Hill. Graham came into her life at a desperate time, then vanished. But Sherrill could not forget the handsome stranger who captured her heart. 07-0303-0

BUILDING YOUR SELF-IMAGE by Josh McDowell and Don Stewart. Here are practical answers to help you overcome your fears, anxieties, and lack of self-confidence. Learn how God's higher image of who you are can take root in your heart and mind. 07-1395-8

THE CHILD WITHIN by Mari Hanes. The author shares insights she gained from God's Word during her own pregnancy, identifying areas of stress, offering concrete data about the birth process, and pointing to God's promises to lead those who are with young. 07-0219-0

CHRISTIANITY: THE FAITH THAT MAKES SENSE by Dennis McCallum. Ideal for new teachers and group study, this readable apologetic presents a clear, rational defense for Christianity to those unfamiliar with the Bible and challenges readers to meet Christ personally. 07-0525-4

COME BEFORE WINTER AND SHARE MY HOPE by Charles R. Swindoll. A collection of brief vignettes offering hope and the assurance that adversity and despair are temporary setbacks we can overcome! 07-0477-0

DAWN OF THE MORNING by Grace Livingston Hill. Dawn Rensselaer is a runaway bride, fleeing a man she was tricked into marrying. But is she also running away from love? 07-0530-0

Other Living Books Best-sellers

DR. DOBSON ANSWERS YOUR QUESTIONS by Dr. James Dobson. In this convenient reference book, renowned author Dr. James Dobson addresses heartfelt concerns on many topics, including questions on marital relationships, infant care, child discipline, home management, and others. 07-0580-7

DR. DOBSON ANSWERS YOUR QUESTIONS: RAISING CHILDREN by Dr. James Dobson. A renowned authority on child-rearing offers his expertise on the spiritual training of children, sex education, discipline, coping with adolescence, and more. 07-1104-1

THE EFFECTIVE FATHER by Gordon MacDonald. A practical study of effective fatherhood based on biblical principles. 07-0669-2

FOR MEN ONLY edited by J. Allan Petersen. This book deals with topics of concern to every man: the business world, marriage, fathering, spiritual goals, and problems of living as a Christian in a secular world. 07-0892-X

FOR WOMEN ONLY by Evelyn R. and J. Allan Petersen. This balanced, entertaining, and diversified treatment covers all the aspects of womanhood. 07-0897-0

GIVERS, TAKERS, AND OTHER KINDS OF LOVERS by Josh McDowell and Paul Lewis. Bypassing generalities about love and sex, this book answers the basics: Whatever happened to sexual freedom? Do men respond differently than women? Here are straight answers about God's plan for love and sexuality. 07-1031-2

HINDS' FEET ON HIGH PLACES by Hannah Hurnard. A classic allegory of a journey toward faith that has sold more than a million copies! 07-1429-6

HOW TO BE HAPPY THOUGH MARRIED by Tim LaHaye. A valuable resource that tells how to develop physical, mental, and spiritual harmony in marriage. 07-1499-7

JOHN, SON OF THUNDER by Ellen Gunderson Traylor. In this saga of adventure, romance, and discovery, travel with John—the disciple whom Jesus loved—down desert paths, through the courts of the Holy City, and to the foot of the cross as he leaves his luxury as a privileged son of Israel for the bitter hardship of his exile on Patmos. 07-1903-4

Other Living Books Best-sellers

LIFE IS TREMENDOUS! by Charlie "Tremendous" Jones. Believing that enthusiasm makes the difference, Jones shows how anyone can be happy, involved, relevant, productive, healthy, and secure in the midst of a high-pressure, commercialized society. 07-2184-5

MORE THAN A CARPENTER by Josh McDowell. A hard-hitting book for people who are skeptical about Jesus' deity, his resurrection, and his claim on their lives. 07-4552-3

QUICK TO LISTEN, SLOW TO SPEAK by Robert E. Fisher. Families are shown how to express love to one another by developing better listening skills, finding ways to disagree without arguing, and using constructive criticism. 07-5111-6

REASONS by Josh McDowell and Don Stewart. In a convenient question-and-answer format, the authors address many of the commonly asked questions about the Bible and evolution. 07-5287-2

RUTH, A LOVE STORY by Ellen Gunderson Traylor. Though the pain of separation and poverty would come upon her, Ruth was to become part of the very fulfillment of prophecy—and find true love as well. A biblical novel. 07-5809-9

THE SECRET OF LOVING by Josh McDowell. McDowell explores the values and qualities that will help both the single and married reader to be the right person for someone else. He offers a fresh perspective for evaluating and improving the reader's love life. 07-5845-5

THE STORY FROM THE BOOK. From Adam to Armageddon, this book captures the full sweep of the Bible's content in abridged, chronological form. Based on *The Book*, the best-selling, popular edition of *The Living Bible*. 07-6677-6

STRIKE THE ORIGINAL MATCH by Charles Swindoll. Swindoll draws on the best marriage survival guide—the Bible—and his 35 years of marriage to show couples how to survive, flex, grow, forgive, and keep romance alive in their marriage. 07-6445-5

THE STRONG-WILLED CHILD by Dr. James Dobson. With practical solutions and humorous anecdotes, Dobson shows how to discipline an assertive child without breaking his spirit. Parents will learn to overcome feelings of defeat or frustration by setting boundaries and taking action. 07-5924-9

Other Living Books Best-sellers

SUCCESS! THE GLENN BLAND METHOD by Glenn Bland. The author shows how to set goals and make plans that really work. His ingredients of success include spiritual, financial, educational, and recreational balances. 07-6689-X

TRANSFORMED TEMPERAMENTS by Tim LaHaye. An analysis of Abraham, Moses, Peter, and Paul, whose strengths and weaknesses were made effective when transformed by God. 07-7304-7

THROUGH GATES OF SPLENDOR by Elisabeth Elliot. This unforgettable story of five men who braved the Auca Indians has become one of the most famous missionary books of all time. 07-7151-6

WHAT WIVES WISH THEIR HUSBANDS KNEW ABOUT WOMEN by Dr. James Dobson. The best-selling author of *Dare to Discipline* and *The Strong-Willed Child* brings us this vital book that speaks to the unique emotional needs and aspirations of today's woman. An immensely practical, interesting guide. 07-7896-0

WHY YOU ACT THE WAY YOU DO by Tim LaHaye. Discover how your temperament affects your work, emotions, spiritual life, and relationships, and learn how to make improvements. 07-8212-7

You can find Tyndale books at fine bookstores everywhere. If you are unable to find these titles at your local bookstore, you may write for ordering information to:

Tyndale House Publishers
Tyndale Family Products Dept.
Box 448
Wheaton, IL 60189